ADVANCE PRAISE FOR

Ben Carniol has long been cial policy debates as an educator and social activist. Now he's written a powerful memoir that tells the harrowing tale of how he survived the Holocaust in hiding as a child in Belgium and later rediscovered his Jewish roots as an adolescent growing up in Ottawa. It's a deeply moving story, and it sheds light on his lifelong journey advancing social justice causes.

Linda McQuaig, journalist and author

This memoir tells of a journey. Ben recounts his experiences as a survivor of the Holocaust. It is a story full of love, tragedy, grief, loss, hope, power and healing in which kindness remains an important human trait. This is a story that draws the reader into a journey full of spirit, transformation and hope. I have a deep respect and love for the work of Ben Carniol. This memoir is well worth reading.

Minogiizhigokwe, Dr. Kathy Absolon, author of *Kaandossiwin: How We Come to Know, Indigenous Re-Search Methodologies*

Ben Carniol's memoir, *Hide and Seek*, recounts the powerful story of a young boy left by his parents in the care of a non-Jewish couple in Belgium during the Shoah. This act doubtless saved Ben's life, and after the war, Ben was able to reclaim his Jewish identity. If this poignant account were all this book was, that would be enough. But *Hide and Seek* goes much further. Ben explores his own personal and professional journey as an adult into a life and career dedicated to social justice. He considers deeply the ways in which his own personal Shoah story led him to activism on behalf of the disadvantaged, which has animated his entire adult life. This book is an important reflection on loss, trauma, identity, politics and faith.

Rabbi Edward Elkin, First Narayever Congregation, Toronto

In 2020, Ben Carniol shared a snippet of his history in my Toronto living room as part of an Israeli program called Zikaron BaSalon. The program features Holocaust survivors sharing their histories and stories, face to face, in private settings. Ben spoke with gentleness, empathy and humour. Listeners were spellbound, not just by his history, but by his life-affirming response to trauma. He told us that evening that it was the first time he had publicly shared his story in such detail. "Ben," I said to him afterwards, "I believe you have a book in there." How lucky are we as readers that we get to discover the full, complex portrait of his experience and hear his voice in this memoir. It is a miracle worth savouring, one page at a time.

Dr. Lesley Simpson

Ben Carniol's trajectory could have been quite different had he not listened to his heart. Driven by the need to alleviate suffering, he immersed himself in the key historical struggles of his time with a humble openness to learning, reassessing his identity along the way as partner, father, ally, settler, citizen and educator. Fundamental to his journey is his identity as a Holocaust survivor. In his ultimate act of courage, he faces the unimaginable loss of his parents, family and community in the genocide, releasing his grief and abandonment, leading to a reimagined faith rooted in "rebellious empathy." His profound commitment to ally himself with struggles for social justice reflects a life-affirming view of human nature founded on the values of cooperation, kindness and respect for diversity. Ben's story urges us to challenge the dehumanizing forces that threaten empathy and to embrace the power of our shared humanity.

Luisa Quarta, MSW

Ben Carniol, seven years old, on learning that he will never again see his beloved parents, seeks comfort at a tiny nearby stream. He places his feet in the clean water, its gentleness washing over his toes. In that moment Ben concludes, just as the stream flows on, so too will his life. Thanks to many courageous people, Ben emerges from the Holocaust and survives to carry on. With great eloquence, inspired by such teachers as Rabbi Abraham Joshua Heschel and Martin Luther King, Jr., Ben calls the reader to action, to work for a world that accepts everyone, human and non-human.

Leonard Molczadski

Ben Carniol, now a retired professor of social work, was rescued by a Belgian-Catholic couple during the Holocaust. In this book, Ben shares his long journey toward healing as he emerged from a traumatic childhood to lead a life that has been devoted to helping others. He gained strength from the love he experienced from his Belgian rescuers, from his Canadian adoptive family, from memories of his birth parents, and later from his wife and daughters, his Jewish heritage — which he reaccepted in Canada — and through activism. Ben has been a major contributor to the development of social work education, including for the First Nations people in Canada. Ben shares with readers the story of a life devoted to seeking social justice and peace, including in Israel/Palestine. A rare person has provided us with an inspiring model opposing the powerful forces that dehumanize people and indeed threaten to destroy the whole world.

Dr. Yisrael Elliot Cohen, prize-winning translator of Holocaust novel *Devilspel*, former staff member of International Institute for Holocaust Research at Yad Vashem

With great humility and deep reflection, Ben has skillfully interwoven the spiritual, emotional and intellectual facets of his life. For Ben, social justice can only be effective and sustainable through the integration of one's inner world and one's external realities. Ben's vision and wisdom are guiding lights in my own social work practice.

Judy Tsao, Frontline Worker, Community Health Centre, Toronto, Ontario

Hide and Seek

THE AZRIELI SERIES OF HOLOCAUST SURVIVOR MEMOIRS: PUBLISHED TITLES

ENGLISH TITLES

Judy Abrams, *Tenuous Threads*/ Eva Felsenburg Marx, *One of the Lucky Ones*
Amek Adler, *Six Lost Years*
Ferenc Andai, *In the Hour of Fate and Danger*
Molly Applebaum, *Buried Words: The Diary of Molly Applebaum*
Claire Baum, *The Hidden Package*
Bronia and Joseph Beker, *Joy Runs Deeper*
Tibor Benyovits, *Unsung Heroes*
Pinchas Eliyahu Blitt, *A Promise of Sweet Tea*
Max Bornstein, *If Home Is Not Here*
Sonia Caplan, *Passport to Reprieve*
Felicia Carmelly, *Across the Rivers of Memory*
Stefan A. Carter, *A Symphony of Remembrance*
Judy Cohen, *A Cry in Unison*
Tommy Dick, *Getting Out Alive*
Marie Doduck, *A Childhood Unspoken*
Marian Domanski, *Fleeing from the Hunter*
Anita Ekstein, *Always Remember Who You Are*
Margalith Esterhuizen, *A Light in the Clouds*
Leslie Fazekas, *In Dreams Together: The Diary of Leslie Fazekas*
John Freund, *Spring's End*
Susan Garfield, *Too Many Goodbyes: The Diaries of Susan Garfield*
Myrna Goldenberg (Editor), *Before All Memory Is Lost: Women's Voices from the Holocaust*
René Goldman, *A Childhood Adrift*
Elly Gotz, *Flights of Spirit*
Ibolya Grossman and Andy Réti, *Stronger Together*
Pinchas Gutter, *Memories in Focus*

Anna Molnár Hegedűs, *As the Lilacs Bloomed*
Rabbi Pinchas Hirschprung, *The Vale of Tears*
Bronia Jablon, *A Part of Me*
Helena Jockel, *We Sang in Hushed Voices*
Jack Klajman, *The Smallest Hope*
Eddie Klein, *Inside the Walls*
Michael Kutz, *If, By Miracle*
Ferenc Laczó (Editor), *Confronting Devastation: Memoirs of Holocaust Survivors from Hungary*
Eva Lang, David Korn and Fishel Philip Goldig, *At Great Risk: Memoirs of Rescue during the Holocaust*
Nate Leipciger, *The Weight of Freedom*
Alex Levin, *Under the Yellow & Red Stars*
Rachel Lisogurski and Chana Broder, *Daring to Hope*
Fred Mann, *A Drastic Turn of Destiny*
Michael Mason, *A Name Unbroken*
Leslie Meisels with Eva Meisels, *Suddenly the Shadow Fell*
Leslie Mezei, *A Tapestry of Survival*
Muguette Myers, *Where Courage Lives*
David Newman, *Hope's Reprise*
Arthur Ney, *W Hour*
Felix Opatowski, *Gatehouse to Hell*
Marguerite Élias Quddus, *In Hiding*
Maya Rakitova, *Behind the Red Curtain*
Henia Reinhartz, *Bits and Pieces*
Betty Rich, *Little Girl Lost*
Paul-Henri Rips, *E/96: Fate Undecided*
Margrit Rosenberg Stenge, *Silent Refuge*
Steve Rotschild, *Traces of What Was*

Judith Rubinstein, *Dignity Endures*
Martha Salcudean, *In Search of Light*
Kitty Salsberg and Ellen Foster, *Never Far Apart*
Morris Schnitzer, *Escape from the Edge*
Joseph Schwarzberg, *Dangerous Measures*
Zuzana Sermer, *Survival Kit*
Rachel Shtibel, *The Violin*/ Adam Shtibel, *A Child's Testimony*
Maxwell Smart, *Chaos to Canvas*
Gerta Solan, *My Heart Is At Ease*
Zsuzsanna Fischer Spiro, *In Fragile Moments*/ Eva Shainblum, *The Last Time*
George Stern, *Vanished Boyhood*
Willie Sterner, *The Shadows Behind Me*
Ann Szedlecki, *Album of My Life*
William Tannenzapf, *Memories from the Abyss*/ Renate Krakauer, *But I Had a Happy Childhood*
Elsa Thon, *If Only It Were Fiction*
Agnes Tomasov, *From Generation to Generation*
Joseph Tomasov, *From Loss to Liberation*
Leslie Vertes, *Alone in the Storm*
Anka Voticky, *Knocking on Every Door*
Sam Weisberg, *Carry the Torch*/ Johnny Jablon, *A Lasting Legacy*

TITRES FRANÇAIS

Judy Abrams, *Retenue par un fil*/ Eva Felsenburg Marx, *Une question de chance*
Amek Adler, *Six années volées*
Molly Applebaum, *Les Mots enfouis: Le Journal de Molly Applebaum*
Claire Baum, *Le Colis caché*
Bronia et Joseph Beker, *Plus forts que le malheur*
Max Bornstein, *Citoyen de nulle part*
Tommy Dick, *Objectif: survivre*
Marian Domanski, *Traqué*
John Freund, *La Fin du printemps*
Myrna Goldenberg (Éditrice), *Un combat singulier: Femmes dans la tourmente de l'Holocauste*
René Goldman, *Une enfance à la dérive*
Pinchas Gutter, *Dans la chambre noire*
Anna Molnár Hegedűs, *Pendant la saison des lilas*
Helena Jockel, *Nous chantions en sourdine*
Michael Kutz, *Si, par miracle*
Eva Lang, Fishel Philip Goldig, David Korn, *Un si grand péril : mémoires de sauvetage durant l'Holocauste*
Nate Leipciger, *Le Poids de la liberté*
Alex Levin, *Étoile jaune, étoile rouge*
Fred Mann, *Un terrible revers de fortune*
Michael Mason, *Au fil d'un nom*
Leslie Meisels, *Soudain, les ténèbres*
Muguette Myers, *Les Lieux du courage*
Arthur Ney, *L'Heure W*
Felix Opatowski, *L'Antichambre de l'enfer*
Marguerite Élias Quddus, *Cachée*
Henia Reinhartz, *Fragments de ma vie*
Betty Rich, *Seule au monde*
Paul-Henri Rips, *Matricule E/96*
Margrit Rosenberg Stenge, *Le Refuge du silence*
Steve Rotschild, *Sur les traces du passé*
Kitty Salsberg et Ellen Foster, *Unies dans l'épreuve*
Zuzana Sermer, *Trousse de survie*
Rachel Shtibel, *Le Violon*/ Adam Shtibel, *Témoignage d'un enfant*
George Stern, *Une jeunesse perdue*
Willie Sterner, *Les Ombres du passé*
Ann Szedlecki, *L'Album de ma vie*
William Tannenzapf, *Souvenirs de l'abîme*/ Renate Krakauer, *Le Bonheur de l'innocence*
Elsa Thon, *Que renaisse demain*
Agnes Tomasov, *De génération en génération*
Leslie Vertes, *Seul dans la tourmente*
Anka Voticky, *Frapper à toutes les portes*
Sam Weisberg, *Passeur de mémoire*/ Johnny Jablon, *Souvenez-vous*

Hide and Seek
In Pursuit of Justice
Ben Carniol

FIRST EDITION
Copyright © 2023 The Azrieli Foundation and others. All rights reserved.

Copyright in individual works, parts of works and/or photographs included within this published work is also claimed by individuals and entities, and effort has been made to obtain the relevant permissions. All requests and questions concerning copyright and reproduction of all or part of this publication may be directed to The Azrieli Foundation. We welcome any information regarding references or credits so as to correct subsequent editions.

THE AZRIELI FOUNDATION · www.azrielifoundation.org

Cover design by Endpaper Studio · Cover image courtesy of WorshipStudioWorks · Book design by Mark Goldstein · Interior map by Julie Witmer Custom Map Design and Eric Leinberger · Translations of letters on pages 143–173 by Brian Cohen, Rhona Carniol and Aliza Krefetz · Endpaper maps by Martin Gilbert.

LIBRARY AND ARCHIVES CANADA CATALOGUING IN PUBLICATION

Hide and seek: in pursuit of justice/ Ben Carniol.
    Carniol, Ben, author. Azrieli Foundation, publisher.
The Azrieli series of Holocaust survivor memoirs; XV
Includes index.
Canadiana (print) 20230515371 · Canadiana (ebook) 20230515436
ISBN 9781998880096 (softcover) · ISBN 9781998880102 (PDF)
ISBN 9781998880119 (EPUB)

LCSH: Jews — Belgium — Biography. LCSH: Hidden children (Holocaust) — Belgium — Biography. LCGFT: Autobiographies.

LCC DS 135.B43 C37 2023   DDC 940.53/18092—dc23

PRINTED IN CANADA

The Azrieli Foundation's Holocaust Survivor Memoirs Program

Naomi Azrieli, Publisher

Jody Spiegel, Program Director
Arielle Berger, Managing Editor
Catherine Person, Manager and Editor of French Translations
Catherine Aubé, Editor of French Translations
Matt Carrington, Editor
Devora Levin, Editor and Special Projects Coordinator
Aefa Mulholland, Editorial Assistant and Program Coordinator
Carson Phillips, Manager of Academic Initiatives
Marc-Olivier Cloutier, Manager of Education Initiatives
Nadine Auclair, Educator
Michelle Sadowski, Educator
Elizabeth Banks, Curator and Archivist

Mark Goldstein, Art Director

Contents

Series Preface	xv
Editorial Note	xvii
Introduction *by Rebecca Clifford*	xix
Map	xxxi
Opening Words	1
Separation	3
Explosions and Fears of War	9
More War, More Fear	13
Renewal	17
My Re-emerging Jewish Self	23
Responding to Grief	31
Echoes of Antisemitism	35
Awakenings	39
Quest for Meaning	45
Community Activism	49
Voter Registration	53
Worlds Apart: The Vietnam War and Memories of Belgium	61
Anti-Poverty Activism	67
Joys and Challenges	75
My Inner Life Grows	81

Indigenous Resistance	85
Human Nature and Suffering	89
Frantz and Minn	95
Facing the Holocaust	99
Revisiting the Past	105
A Moment of Remembering	109
Decolonizing Social Work Education	113
Expanding the Circle	121
Threats to Empathy	129
Calls to Action	135
Miracles	139
Correspondence	143
Acknowledgements	175
Glossary	179
Photographs	189
Index	215

Series Preface:
In their own words...

In telling these stories, the writers have liberated themselves. For so many years we did not speak about it, even when we became free people living in a free society. Now, when at last we are writing about what happened to us in this dark period of history, knowing that our stories will be read and live on, it is possible for us to feel truly free. These unique historical documents put a face on what was lost, and allow readers to grasp the enormity of what happened to six million Jews — one story at a time.

> David J. Azrieli, C.M., C.Q., M.Arch
> Holocaust survivor and founder, The Azrieli Foundation

Since the end of World War II, approximately 40,000 Jewish Holocaust survivors have immigrated to Canada. Who they are, where they came from, what they experienced and how they built new lives for themselves and their families are important parts of our Canadian heritage. The Azrieli Foundation's Holocaust Survivor Memoirs Program was established in 2005 to preserve and share the memoirs written by those who survived the twentieth-century Nazi genocide of the Jews of Europe and later made their way to Canada. The memoirs encourage readers to engage thoughtfully and critically with the complexities of the Holocaust and to create meaningful connections with the lives of survivors.

Millions of individual stories are lost to us forever. By preserving the stories written by survivors and making them widely available to a broad audience, the Azrieli Foundation's Holocaust Survivor Memoirs Program seeks to sustain the memory of all those who perished at the hands of hatred, abetted by indifference and apathy. The personal accounts of those who survived against all odds are as different as the people who wrote them, but all demonstrate the courage, strength, wit and luck that it took to prevail and survive in such terrible adversity. The memoirs are also moving tributes to people — strangers and friends — who risked their lives to help others, and who, through acts of kindness and decency in the darkest of moments, frequently helped the persecuted maintain faith in humanity and courage to endure. These accounts offer inspiration to all, as does the survivors' desire to share their experiences so that new generations can learn from them.

The Holocaust Survivor Memoirs Program collects, archives and publishes select survivor memoirs and makes the print editions available free of charge to educational institutions and Holocaust-education programs across Canada. They are also available for sale online to the general public. All revenues to the Azrieli Foundation from the sales of the Azrieli Series of Holocaust Survivor Memoirs go toward the publishing and educational work of the memoirs program.

∼

The Azrieli Foundation would like to express appreciation to the following people for their invaluable efforts in producing this book: Niesha Davis, Mark Duffus (Maracle Inc.), Jess Herdman, Kaitlin Littlechild, Alison Strobel and the team at Second Story Press.

Editorial Note

The following memoir contains terms, concepts and historical references that may be unfamiliar to the reader. English translations of foreign-language words and terms have been added to the text, and parentheses have been used to include the names and locations of present-day towns and cities when place names have changed. The editors of this memoir have worked to maintain the author's voice and stay true to the original narrative while maintaining historical accuracy. Explanatory footnotes have been added for clarification or to provide key information for understanding the text. General information on major organizations, significant historical events and people, geographical locations, religious and cultural terms, and foreign-language words and expressions that will help give context to the events described in the text can be found in the glossary beginning on page 179.

Introduction

Ben Carniol's life story, as you encounter it in these pages, is remarkable, moving and unique. At the same time, however, there are commonalities that link his experiences very strongly to those of other child survivors of the Holocaust. By way of introduction to his memoir, I would like to highlight some of the ways in which his story — individual as every life story is — nonetheless resonates with the wider experiences of children who lived through the Holocaust, and who have gone on to lead rich lives in the nearly eighty years since the end of World War II.

Ben was born in 1937 in Teplitz-Schönau (modern day Teplice, Czech Republic), in the border region called the Sudetenland. The Sudetenland was an early target of Nazi imperial and expansionist policy, claimed by Germany in October 1938, nearly a year before the start of the war. The region was thus a bellwether that suggested what would come for many other parts of central and eastern Europe soon afterward. Ben's parents were clear-eyed enough to realize the danger and flee the region for Belgium in 1938. This was a forward-thinking decision, and they of course had no way of knowing that Belgium, too, would soon be a place that was not safe for families of Jewish origin.

Ben himself, however, was unaware of the danger facing his family, as was the case for many very young children during the Holocaust.

Only five years old in 1942, when the situation began to look increasingly fraught for Jewish people living in occupied Belgium, Ben might have sometimes noticed his parents' growing anxiety, but this did not mean that he was afraid for himself or for his mother and father at this moment of very real danger. He continued to play as all children play. He thought little of it when his parents arranged to "go on a vacation" and leave him with Minn and Frantz Vandenheuvel. He had no way of knowing that Minn and Frantz were in fact part of the Belgian underground resistance movement, and that his parents had decided to leave him in the care of this couple while they fled. It is worth taking a moment to appreciate the remarkable bravery of parents who left their young children in the care of non-Jewish near-strangers in the hopes of one day being able to rebuild their families. For Ben's parents, as for so many other parents who made similar choices, the gamble often paid off in part. Many small children survived in this way. Many parents did not, and Ben's parents were among them.

Ben spent the rest of the war years in hiding as a Catholic, a very common experience among child Holocaust survivors. Living with Minn and Frantz in the small village of Baudour, he was baptized in the village church, attended a Catholic primary school and went along to Mass with Minn on most Sundays. "I had no awareness of pretending to be Catholic," he recalls; he *was* Catholic, but he was also aware of his Jewish origins. He was simply living in accordance with the practices in the village, blending in while still conscious of being different, enjoying his warm relationship with Minn even as he began to realize that his parents had been away on their "vacation" for far too long.

In this, Ben's experience in hiding was typical of that of many child survivors, especially those hidden with Christian families in western European countries such as Belgium, France or the Netherlands. In these countries, children were generally placed with Christian host families either directly by their parents or by clandestine aid organizations such as the Œuvre de secours aux enfants (OSE). Children were also hidden in religious institutions, particularly Catholic convents. Their experiences could be lonely and isolating, and there were some who fell prey to abusers, but many children formed deep and loving bonds with their wartime host families, just as Ben did with Minn. For very young children, the host family might have been the only family they could remember at all; indeed, for such a young child, Ben is unusual in having some clear memories of his birth parents. Many children felt comfortable with their host families and they learned to be Catholic, often forgetting that they had ever been anything else. This meant that the end of the war, far from being a moment of liberation, was often a profoundly disrupting shock to hidden Jewish children. Ben recalls the moment as joyous, but for many of his peers it brought with it changes that jolted them out of fairly stable wartime lives.

The end of the war raised the question of where hidden Jewish children belonged. For Jewish religious and institutional leaders, this issue seemed like a profound crisis. In 1939, there had been an estimated 1.5 million Jewish children living in continental Europe. By 1945, the international relief organization United Nations Relief and Rehabilitation Administration (UNRRA) estimated that only 150,000 of these children remained, with an additional 30,000 alive who had fled into the Soviet Union or left continental Europe by other routes. An entire generation had been lost, and Jewish leaders were preoccupied with salvaging what remained. From their perspective, reclaiming for Judaism those children who were living as Catholics was a priority. This goal, however, sometimes clashed with the desires of children to stay with their wartime host families. Some children had to be removed by force. Some were returned to surviving parents or relatives who they could no longer remember and with whom they often no longer even shared a common language. Others were sent to Jewish care homes, effectively to be "re-Judaicized" through collective living.

Ben's experience here was both typical and unusual. It was typical in that although he continued to live with Minn and Frantz in Belgium until 1947, he was not simply allowed to go on living as a Catholic boy in a small Belgian village; his relatives in Ottawa claimed him. There are some unusual aspects to his story here: the first is that he does not remember his uprooting to Ottawa as particularly disruptive or upsetting, the second is that Minn and Frantz were able to relocate to Canada shortly after he did (which undoubtedly made the transition easier to bear), and the third is that Ben's family desperately wanted to have him migrate sooner but were stymied by Canada's highly restrictive immigration laws. Their support and care can be seen in the fascinating collection of letters that can be found at the end of this book.

In moving to Ottawa, Ben — like the majority of child Holocaust survivors — entered a postwar global diaspora. As surviving family members and Jewish aid agencies claimed these children, survivor children fanned out to new homes across the globe, particularly in the Anglo-American world and in British Mandate Palestine (Israel after 1948). These children found themselves having to make sense of new families, homes, languages, cultures and citizenships. Ben recalls a fairly smooth transition as he left his provincial home in Belgium and found himself living with his extended family (his aunt, cousins and maternal grandparents) in Ottawa. But for many child survivors, entering this shuffle across the globe was deeply destabilizing.

One noteworthy incident stands out in his recollections: Upon arrival in his new home in Ottawa, Ben tried to hang a cross that Minn had given him above his bed. What made the incident so evocative was his maternal grandfather's furious reaction to this Christian symbol. The rest of Ben's Ottawa family convinced the grandfather to simply let the cross remain for the time being: "eventually, someone took the cross down, and I hardly noticed that it was gone." This small but significant moment revealed ongoing conflicts in Ben's identity, and here we see further synergies with the experiences of many hidden children. Young children in hiding had years in which to imbibe the lesson that being Jewish was dangerous. They were adept at hiding their Jewish roots. They often adopted non-Jewish names. Postwar attempts to "re-Judaicize" hidden children simply drove many children to conceal their ongoing emotional connections to Catholicism. Paul Friedman, a psychiatrist who undertook a study of the psychological condition of child survivors living in displaced persons camps[1] in the early postwar period, described how attempts to steer children back toward Judaism were creating emotional conflicts in many survivor children. Talking with a Jewish youth leader in charge of a group of child survivors in a displaced persons camp in 1946, Friedman wrote:

She believed that all the children's conflicts had been solved and that she had been successful in bringing them back to a faith in Judaism. When I pointed out that the children still kept crosses and prayer books underneath their pillows, she brushed this aside as an innocuous addiction to souvenirs. Unfortunately, after having discussed this particular problem with many of these children, I found it impossible to be as optimistic. Many of them had deep conflicts concerning their Jewishness, which for years had been a secret whose betrayal might mean death.[2]

What was exceptional in Ben's account was his new family's willingness to let him make his own transition back to Jewishness when he chose to of his own accord and felt ready. This was rare for the time.

Viewing his childhood past through adult eyes, Ben acknowledges how patient and understanding his Ottawa family were, but this

---

[1] Facilities set up by the Allied authorities and the UNRRA in October 1945 to resolve the refugee crisis that arose at the end of World War II. The camps provided temporary shelter and assistance to the millions of people who had been displaced from their home countries as a result of the war and helped them prepare for resettlement.

[2] Paul Friedman, 'The Road Back for the DPs: Healing the Psychological Scars of Nazism', *Commentary*, December 1948.

does not mean that there was necessarily an open discussion about the past in his new household. He recalls that he sometimes tried to ask his aunt (now Mom) and his cousins (now his siblings) what had happened to his birth parents, but "I quickly learned not to ask." Reflecting on his younger self, Ben recognizes that he was struggling to process his grief and his guilt — and that his new family was equally grieving. He had lost his mother and father, but for his maternal family, his mother had been a beloved daughter, sister and aunt.

Part of what made it so difficult for the family to grieve was the fact that so little was known about Ben's parents' deaths. Ben recalls that he learned about their deaths in stages; he writes: "I continued to hope well into my teens that one day the doorbell would ring, announcing that they were back." This was an extremely common experience for Holocaust survivors, and it was not an unreasonable wish. Ben accounts for it by explaining: "For years, I avoided facing what my parents and others had experienced in Nazi captivity." But denial was only a part of this dynamic. For many Holocaust survivors, the difficulty in grieving for murdered loved ones was compounded by the fact that in the early postwar years and even decades, relatively little was known about the Nazi genocidal system. Many relatives of the victims had very little idea of what had happened to their loved ones until they applied to the West German indemnification program for compensation. (The program was launched in the mid-1950s, but the first large batches of applications were only processed in the late 1950s and early 1960s). Through the indemnification program, many survivors received paper evidence of their loved ones' deportations, imprisonments and deaths for the first time — more than a decade after the war's end.

To further complicate matters, survivors continued to show up alive for the best part of that postwar decade. To put Ben's hope that his parents would one day ring the doorbell in perspective, we might look to the case of an orphanage for child Holocaust survivors in the village of Lingfield in the south of England. Most of the children brought to Lingfield were believed to be orphaned, yet their parents continually showed up. The first set of parents — a surviving mother and father — were located in 1946. The last, a surviving mother, was not located until 1952. In the intervening years, what child at this one small orphanage would not have hoped against hope that their mother or father might indeed be found alive? This pattern was repeated in every one of the hundreds of care homes for child survivors and in every household where surviving relatives had no definitive proof of their loved ones' deaths. If they struggled to mourn, it was caused as much by a terribly long period of uncertainty as by denial of the horror behind these murders.

Memory — especially traumatic memory — is unpredictable. The past can rear up and overwhelm us in the midst of otherwise tranquil daily moments. One terrifying moment that Ben recalls happened when he had grown into a young father with two small daughters. Playing with his children one day, he had a vision when his baby daughter Naomi opened her mouth to laugh:

As Naomi's mouth opened wide with laughter, I could see the full range of her new teeth. They were tiny, white and gorgeous. But then I got a shock. My imagination was triggered, and at first, I wasn't sure what I was seeing, but as I focused my vision, I was repelled. I saw the outline of several corpses and skeletons with white bones strewn on the ground. They I saw a close-up of two corpses, partly covered with soil, each with a row of white-grey teeth. I sensed that these were the teeth of my parents.

Across the world, around the same time, child Holocaust survivors were grappling with similar frightening experiences. The birth of children often provoked thoughts, consciously or unconsciously, about lost mothers and fathers. Some child survivors worried that because they had lost their own birth parents, perhaps they would fail to be good parents in return. Some found that when their children were the age that they had been when they last saw their own parents, a strange fear gripped them, provoking nightmares and bringing to mind lives lost as much as new lives created. Some even went through periods of struggling to hold or touch their own children, beset by waves of latent fears. No psychologists at the time recognized that this was a common occurrence, even those who worked directly with child survivors. One wonders how much Ben's anxiety might have been eased had he known that he was not alone in his terrifying experience.

Indeed, Ben recalls that he was not able to fully grieve for his lost parents until the 1990s, when his aunt passed away. "I had consciously and unconsciously repressed, evaded and postponed grieving for them," he writes. "My fear had blocked me." Nearly fifty years after the war's end, he at last felt ready to allow himself to visualize their deaths, but also to search his mind for memories of their lives. He thought about how they might have resisted their murders and realized that his own life had been filled with similar acts of resistance aimed at an "undoing of the violations caused by racism." Ben suggests that it was his own fear that stopped this from happening earlier, but he is perhaps too hard on himself here. The truth is that this too was a common experience for many child survivors. Just as the birth of children could provoke a reckoning with the past, so too could the death of a parent (birth, foster or adoptive). Many child survivors recall a strange wave of emotions when their parents or parental figures died. They may have found themselves mourning both the parent who had recently died and at the same time the one (or ones) who had been murdered in the Holocaust. Some recall the sense that an obstacle to remembering had been removed, for often parents had tried to protect children from the truth about the past by refusing to talk about it, or even by concealing basic elements of the family story. Others recall feeling that the weight of remembrance landed on their shoulders after a parent died. Ben's reaction to his adoptive mother's death lies somewhere on this spectrum.

There is another reason, however, why Ben was able to see his own past in a new light in the 1990s. Public interest in the genocide grew in Western countries from the 1970s onward but did not really take off until the 1990s. The end of the Cold War played a role in this changing memorial landscape because Cold War allegiances (especially with West Germany) had made it politically difficult to discuss certain aspects of wartime crimes. With the collapse of the Cold War geopolitical system, there was an explosion of public interest in the legacies of World War II atrocities, the Holocaust foremost among these. Ben's period of private mourning, fifty years on, took place in a changed public and collective memorial landscape.

I have saved for the end one of the central elements of Ben's life story: his activism. As readers will discover, Ben has been an advocate for social justice throughout his entire adult life. After gaining a degree in social work from McGill University, Ben moved to the United States, where he became involved in some of the defining mass social movements of the 1960s, including the drive to register Black voters, and protests against the Vietnam War. Later returning to Canada, he devoted himself for decades to the fight for Indigenous rights.

Here again, there are parallels between Ben's story and that of his wider generation. Most child Holocaust survivors were born a bit too early to be comfortably included in the baby boom generation (those children, the key actors in the protest movements that defined the latter half of the 1960s, were generally born after the war ended). Yet sociologists and historians have long noted just how many young activists of the period were Jewish. Ben got involved in registering Black voters in Cleveland. He recalls being "the only White person in the entire crowd" at a rally with Martin Luther King, Jr., in 1967, but if we consider those White students who went to Mississippi to register Black voters in the landmark Freedom Summer of 1964, an astonishing two-thirds were Jewish. And this was not only the case in the United States. The iconic student movement that erupted in France in May 1968 included a notable percentage of student activists from Jewish backgrounds. Why?

As Paul Berman (himself then an activist of Jewish origins) writes:

The parents of those students, some of them, had spent the Nazi era living like hunted animals, fleeing from place to place, taking part in guerrilla actions when they could. Some of them had ended up in the Nazi camps; others, fleeing eastward from Poland, had ended up in the Soviet camps. The oldest among the children were born under extremely grim circumstances. …Solidarity became their religion. They said, in effect: I struggle on behalf of others, therefore I am. They conceived an idea of identity through action.³

We should see Ben's lifelong choice to work on behalf of others as informed by his wartime experiences. This is not to say that choosing activism was a natural or inevitable choice for child Holocaust survivors — most did not take this path — but that for many young Jewish people growing up in the postwar period, the fact that they had witnessed first-hand the sharp end of prejudice and persecution meant that they chose to stand against it. Like Ben, many still do. Their activism reminds us of what happens when racism is unchecked. This is, perhaps, the most powerful message that Ben's memoir has for its readers. It is a message that every reader can understand, and an act of resistance and courage that any reader can embrace.

Rebecca Clifford
Professor of Transnational European History, Durham University, UK
2023

---

3 Paul Berman, *A Tale of Two Utopias: The Political Journey of the Generation of 1968* (New York: Norton, 1996), pp. 31-33.

FURTHER READING

Irving Abella and Harold Troper, *None Is Too Many: Canada and the Jews of Europe, 1933–1948*, 2nd ed. (Toronto: University of Toronto Press, 2012).

Franklin Bialystok, *Delayed Impact: The Holocaust and the Canadian Jewish Community* (Montreal: McGill-Queen's University Press, 2000).

Kerry Bluglass, *Hidden from the Holocaust: Stories of Resilient Children Who Survived and Thrived* (London: Praeger, 2003).

Rebecca Clifford, *Survivors: Children's Lives After the Holocaust* (London: Yale University Press, 2020).

Beth B. Cohen, *Child Survivors of the Holocaust: The Youngest Remnant and the American Experience* (New Brunswick, NJ: Rutgers University Press, 2018).

Debórah Dwork, *Children with a Star: Jewish Youth in Nazi Europe* (New Haven: Yale University Press, 1991).

Suzanne Vromen, *Hidden Children of the Holocaust: Belgian Nuns and their Daring Rescue of Young Jews from the Nazis* (Oxford: Oxford University Press, 2010).

Tara Zahra, *The Lost Children: Reconstructing Europe's Families After World War II* (Cambridge, Mass.: Harvard University Press, 2011).

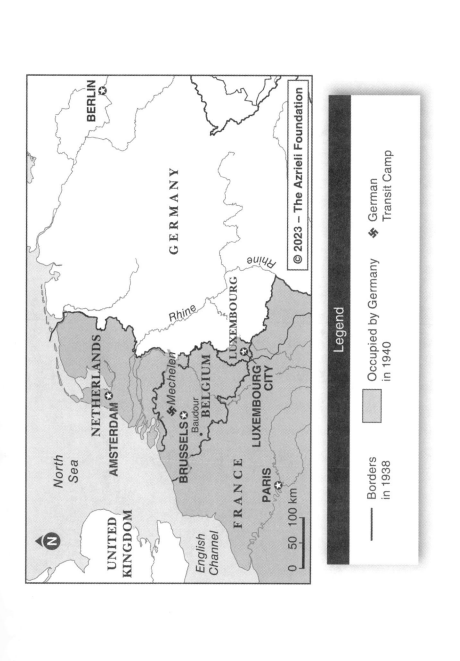

This book is dedicated to my parents, Elsa and Mathias Carniol; to the six million members of my community who were murdered in the Holocaust; to the many social justice advocates, environmentalists, and peace and justice activists who are struggling against nuclear war, genocide and other forms of violence in order to build a world based on justice, democracy, equality, fairness and nonviolence; to the Infinite Spirit, Creator, whose love fashions awe-inspiring worlds; to my immediate family — Rhona, Mira, Naomi, Brian, Noah and Chloe — who show affection and caring in celebrating the joys in my life; and to my many friends, colleagues and mentors who have supported me in my healing journey.

Opening Words

As I reach my eighty-sixth birthday, I now know I could not have written this book about my Holocaust experiences until my later years. I had to first confront my demons of fear, shame and self-blame, which the Nazis generated through their deceptions and their violence. The pangs of my losses were stomped onto my soul; the ear-splitting explosions of the Nazis' genocidal invasions shattered my emotional balance, pummelling my psyche into silence, causing memory lapses that still haunt me today. But because of the courage, empathy and loving support shown by people in my life, I received a miraculous, healing balm, and I was able to fathom and reflect on my past, as well as on the dire threats against all life on this planet.

I face hard questions, hard experiences and hard choices. I write about them using the events of my life as my teachers — teachers that have ignited my rebellious empathy for the many casualties of a multitude of bitter injustices. My rebellious empathy pushes back against the suffering stemming from injustices and against the privilege, power, wealth and other benefits gained from these injustices. While people who gain from injustices often try to convince others that such injustices are natural, inevitable, desirable and untouchable, my empathy toward victims and survivors of injustice has motivated me to join with activists who rebel against normalizing injustice. As a result, I have found myself on a path of seeking justice. It has certainly been exhilarating acting in solidarity with others to protect the sacred gifts bestowed on our beautiful and awe-inspiring planet.

A note about the structure of this memoir: I have intentionally chosen to organize my memoir into twenty-six chapters to reflect the numerical equivalent of God's name, following a mystical method of understanding Jewish texts by interpreting numerical equivalences of Hebrew letters. In many ways, my experiences as a child in the Holocaust and my ongoing quest for justice throughout my life have been defined by seeking the divine in my personal, inner life and in my communal activities, in my spiritual and religious life, and in my pursuit of justice.

Ben Carniol
Toronto
2023

Separation

I was five years old in 1942 when my parents both came to my kindergarten one day to walk me home. I was learning how to speak French in the kindergarten and enjoyed learning a new language because I noticed that the more French I learned, the more I could play with my new friends. My new friends didn't know how to speak German, the language my parents and I spoke at home and had spoken in Czechoslovakia before coming to Belgium.

As we walked the few blocks home, my parents stopped at a park so that I could play in a sandbox. This afternoon, there were no other children playing in the sandbox. My parents had brought my small wooden toys: a red locomotive and a couple of passenger cars that were painted bright yellow. My mother handed me these toys so that I could play my favourite game of choo-choo train in that sandbox.

As I was playing, my father casually told me that he and my mother were planning to go on a vacation. I had no idea what a vacation was, but it was presented to me as a routine thing, and I accepted it. My parents told me we were going for dinner that evening to the Verschuerens — who lived across the street from us — so that we could meet their daughter, Minn, and her husband, Dr. Frantz Vandenheuvel, who would take good care of me until they returned from vacation. I was excited to visit the Verschuerens again because their place was like a magical, luxurious palace to me.

We left the park and walked home to our apartment in a modest building in a quiet residential neighbourhood in Brussels. At home, my mother asked me to wash up and put on the fresh change of clothes she had laid out for me. On the couch there was a small suitcase in which she had packed a few of my clothes. She now packed my favourite toys as well: my small locomotive and two passenger cars. Both of my parents also washed up and changed into fancier clothes — my father now in a suit and my mother in her favourite bright blue dress.

After I finished washing up, my mother held her arms out for a hug, smiling tenderly, and then she held me. My father hugged me less frequently than my mother did, but this time he waited for his turn as well. After giving me an affectionate hug, he said that it was time to go to dinner. We all walked back down the stairs, my father carrying my suitcase, and we crossed the street to our neighbour's house.

When we arrived at the Verschuerens, my father rang the bell, and my mother said to me, "Remember, be a good boy." I smiled at her and nodded: "Yes, Mama." Someone answered the door, and we were invited into the spacious home. Many people had been invited for dinner: Minn's two brothers with their wives and others. I knew one of Minn's brothers, Albert. He had befriended me when I was playing outside on the sidewalk, riding my toy car in front of our apartment. He had invited me to his parents' backyard with its manicured beds of flowers and plants and a narrow pathway where I could ride my toy car.

In the living room, many people were talking at the same time. It was a noisy celebration. This was when I first met Minn and Frantz, who were to be my caregivers. Minn had long black hair and serious eyes that were softened by her wide warm smile. She was much taller than my mother, and Frantz was even taller than Minn. He had blond hair, a thick blond moustache and wore eyeglasses. They were both happily asking me about my favourite games, and I was glad they were friendly.

As we gathered in the dining room, my eyes grew wide with wonder. I had never seen such sparkling silverware at home. It was laid out on a bright tablecloth, along with many tall, shiny glasses. My parents sat on each side of me at the table, and as we waited for the food, my mother leaned over to me and whispered, "We have a surprise treat for you. You'll be going with your caregivers to their home in the countryside by train!" By train! My mother knew I loved playing with my miniature train cars. My parents must have taught me some manners because I managed to wait politely until the meal was almost over. But then I could wait no longer, and I burst out, interrupting whatever conversations were happening: "When can I go on the train?!" After all these years, I can still hear the laughter from the adults at the table. Even then, I did notice there was something off in the laughter, but it was only years later that I understood why it had an edge to it.

After dinner, my parents hugged me again, this time to say goodbye. They assured me that I would be well taken care of by Frantz and Minn. Here is what my parents did not tell me: We were in extreme danger because we were Jewish. We had already fled the Nazis once, leaving Teplitz-Schönau (Teplice-Šanov), Czechoslovakia, where I was born in 1937, to come to Belgium. Teplitz-Schönau was in the Sudetenland, close to Germany, and from 1933 onward, my parents paid attention to how the Nazi regime adopted anti-Jewish laws intended to stigmatize Jews and alienate them from the general population. In 1938, my parents fled Czechoslovakia with me, just before the Night of Broken Glass, or Kristallnacht, when in Germany and Austria, Nazi hoodlums torched hundreds of synagogues and looted thousands of Jewish homes and businesses. About thirty thousand Jewish males were arrested, and most of them were sent to concentration camps, where many became the first victims of the camps.

Unbeknownst to me at that time, this couple, Frantz and Minn, were part of Belgium's secret underground resistance movement that opposed the Nazi occupation. Minn's brother Albert worked for a resistance organization as an expert in forging identification papers. He had produced mine, showing me as a Catholic nephew of Frantz and Minn.

At times, I wonder how my parents coped after they said goodbye to me.

The train ride with Frantz and Minn was short and enjoyable. I imagined myself inside my toy train, being pulled by a powerful steam engine that was taking my caregivers and me and the other passengers toward the small Belgian village of Baudour. We disembarked from the train near Baudour, and a friendly driver met us and drove us to my new home. It was a two-storey red-brick house with a large vegetable garden surrounded by a tall brick wall in the back. Beyond that wall there were small fields that led to a dense forest with many tall trees.

I had my own bedroom on the second floor, next to Frantz and Minn's. The house was much larger and more lavish than the small apartment I had shared with my parents in Brussels. Inside my new home, there was a special play area in the living room next to the fireplace and a large piano that I could sit under. I would spread my toys out over the thick, soft carpet. They had gotten me a Meccano set, with lots of bolts and screws and thin narrow metal bars. I set it up under the piano and enjoyed building structures there.

Soon after I got settled, Frantz told me in a serious tone of voice that I must never, ever tell anyone that I was Jewish. I was to avoid all contact with German soldiers, who sometimes patrolled the village streets. If stopped by a German soldier, I was to keep silent, except to say that I was Frantz and Minn's nephew. Later, I learned that Frantz and Minn could not have children for medical reasons.

I was not hidden in an attic or basement. I lived out in the open like other children, but it was my Jewish identity that was hidden from the people I lived among and from the occupying Nazi army. When I was young, my hair was blond and I had blue eyes, so I could easily pass as non-Jewish, and I blended in with the other children attending school or playing on Baudour's streets.

Minn accompanied me to the village school numerous times until I was able to find my own way. It was about a twenty-minute walk that took me along a quiet unpaved country road, then along a well-worn footpath that passed at the edge of several open fields before entering the edge of the village. From there, I followed a road to the central village square, which was paved with many rounded cobblestones and from which rose a tall and stern grey brick building — the village's Catholic Church. I was baptized in that church. I also went to Mass with Minn most Sundays and attended confession. Minn was a devout Catholic, and she must have been pleased that I embraced her faith.

The village Catholic school was just a few blocks from the village square. There I made new friends and was subjected to strict school discipline, just like the other students. Some of the teacher-nuns carried a long wooden ruler as they taught. If we didn't pay attention, we would get hit on our fingers by those rulers. After I got hit for talking once, I began to escape into my own thoughts and imagination.

During the week, teachers would assign lots of homework, and Frantz and Minn would help me with it. Sometimes the nuns would ask us to draw a detailed picture of a story we were studying at school. Minn would help me draw. We also had to memorize multiplication tables. To me, those tables were a jumble of numbers that were like a giant awful puzzle. Frantz would help me understand the system behind those tables. Frantz and Minn would cheer when I got the right answer. Homework became fun, and I concluded that they were both very smart.

Going to church was easier than doing homework; I only had to imitate what Minn did. I had no awareness of pretending to be Catholic. When going to church, I felt I was Catholic, and I had no sense that being Christian was a different religion than being Jewish. But one time, I did confide in one of my young friends. We were at school when I whispered to him, *Do you know how to keep a secret?* He whispered back, *Of course!* I told him, *I'm Jewish.* He was surprised, and then gave me a huge smile. He whispered: *That's amazing! You're the same religion as Jesus!* He then glanced at me with admiration. I quickly said, *Please tell no one!* He nodded while I put a finger over my mouth. *Your secret is safe with me,* he whispered. As far as I know, he never told anyone. We simply continued our childhood camaraderie and never spoke about it again. I was oblivious to the danger I had put myself in.

After school, it was time for fun. One of my favourite games was hide-and-seek. My classmates and I would hide in the various nooks and crannies of the church when it was empty of adults. My best hiding place was in one of the confession booths. But after hiding there several times, I decided that it was a sin. So, on confession day, when my classmates and I lined up in front of the confession booth, I told the priest that I was very sorry I had hidden in his booth. He asked if I had stolen anything from the church or if I had broken or destroyed anything in the church. I replied that I hadn't and was upset that the priest would even think that I might steal or break something. The priest told me that I was forgiven; I just shouldn't hide there again. I was relieved to be free of sin and became a very happy little boy. I planned how, when I saw my mother, I would tell her the priest had forgiven me. *You see Mama. I was a good boy after all.*

Explosions and Fears of War

I was getting used to my daily routine in Baudour — making new friends, going to school during the week, attending church on Sundays. My caregivers suggested I call them Uncle Frantz and Aunt Minn, which I agreed to do. Meanwhile, the war was intensifying. Unexpected explosions unnerved me.

One time, I was sitting at our kitchen table when a loud blast suddenly blew the kitchen window open, the edge of the window frame narrowly missing my head. Moments later, I saw a huge brown cloud rising from the forest on the other side of the field behind our home. The cloud became so massive that it blocked out the sky as it slowly passed over our house. Soon afterwards, I overheard whispers in the village that the blast had been set off by a secret partisan group, and they had blown up the chemical factory deep inside the forest.

Shortly after that explosion, the Gestapo caught Frantz and threw him into prison because of his involvement in the resistance. Frantz was a scientist working for a chemical factory near Baudour. Much later, after the war, I saw pictures Frantz had drawn of a railway bridge that was to be blown up to disrupt the Nazis' flow of supplies. After Frantz's arrest, Minn became my full-time protector. I sensed that Minn did not want to talk about what had happened to Frantz, but now I feel that her silence may also have been caused by my own fears. I was young, but I knew there were large events happening that

I could not influence. Wave after wave of foreign troops arrived in Belgium, and their army tanks were now controlling Belgium and the streets of the village where I lived. These foreign soldiers were busy with their own goals that I did not understand. I was warned that it was dangerous for me to ask those soldiers what they were doing or why they were here. I was looking for safety, and I found safety in being quiet and not asking any questions like: Why were there explosions? Why was Frantz absent? Why was there a war? Why did the nuns whisper when talking about war? I was thinking and observing but said nothing, asked nothing. The explosions scared me. I knew I could be hurt or killed. I was safer if I did and said nothing. So I became as invisible as a quiet little mouse hiding under the small bushes in the garden.

One day, I saw Minn at the coffee table in the living room, drawing a detailed map of Belgium, outlining its borders and using different coloured pencils to show the country's regions. When she had completed the map, she took off her wedding ring, looped a thin thread through it and held it over the map, moving the thread and ring slowly over its surface. Then she and I noticed that the ring was gently swaying over one particular spot, just above the Belgian city of Mons. She proclaimed, "There he is!" then smiled and said with such certainty that Frantz was all right that I didn't doubt her at all.

Much later, Minn told me that she had found out that Frantz was held by the Gestapo at a prison in Mons. Frantz and Minn occasionally communicated. He would send her clothing for repair, such as a torn handkerchief on which he had threaded a coded pattern that she could decipher. Or he would write on thin cigarette paper in tiny script and sew it into the collar of a shirt that he sent to Minn to wash. The Gestapo found Frantz guilty of espionage and condemned him to death by firing squad. But, Minn learned, they decided not to carry out this penalty because they planned to use his scientific knowledge after they won the war, though they did not tell Frantz of his reprieve.

On another day, when Minn had gone on some errands, I was home with one of my babysitters. Suddenly, there was the sound of an airplane flying so low right above our house that its engines seemed to be screaming inside my ears. I ran to the kitchen window and saw a warplane flying away from us, then veering to the right while losing altitude, a long plume of thick, brownish-black smoke trailing behind it. It looked like a British or American plane had been hit by gunfire. Suddenly it took a nosedive into the ground, and instantly there were ear-splitting explosions that rocked our house. I screamed, then did the worst thing — I ran outside. My babysitter bolted after me, caught up with me in the front of the house, and pushed me down as she rolled on top of me to protect me from flying debris caused by the blast. Fortunately, we escaped injury. That babysitter risked her life to save mine. I don't even know her name.

Soon after, Minn visited Brussels, taking me with her. When we arrived at the train station in Brussels, there were soldiers everywhere, each with a large rifle slung over his shoulder. I knew they were German soldiers because of their distinctively shaped helmets that curved down over their ears and the drab green colour of their military uniforms. I didn't like them. My friends and I would play, pretending to be soldiers with guns. We would shout bang-bang, pretending to kill kids who were pretending to be the enemy. But at the train station, these were real soldiers; I knew they were from the "other side." I didn't like their facial expressions. It was as if they knew they should not be here. There were no smiles, only ugly frowns, made even scarier by the big rifles they were carrying. I didn't like the large size of their guns, knowing they were not make-believe but could kill people right here.

Minn led me on a short walk to a streetcar stop on a wide boulevard near the train station. We were on our way to visit her parents. I had dressed in my Sunday clothing — short pants and a white shirt. Minn too wore her Sunday clothing — a grey suit with an orange kerchief. As we approached the streetcar stop, we saw that a streetcar was already there. German soldiers had set up a military checkpoint right where the streetcar was waiting. As we approached, one of the tall soldiers shouted commands to Minn, me and others who were headed for the streetcar. "No talking! Silence! Stand in a straight line here!" We obeyed. A line formed from the streetcar doors toward the open boulevard.

The passenger line moved slowly as a Nazi soldier checked each person's identification papers before they boarded the streetcar. When it was our turn, the soldier checked the papers that Minn had given him and ordered her to open the small suitcase she was carrying. She obeyed, and he moved one hand over our clothes. He noticed a small bottle holding a dark liquid in the corner of the suitcase and asked her what was in the bottle. "It's medicine for my little boy," she replied. As the soldier asked Minn more questions, I looked away from them toward some soldiers who were standing nearby. Suddenly, I became aware of one soldier who was sitting on a low stool near the back doors of the streetcar. He was totally silent, motionless. He had a full view of us, and in front of him was a very large machine gun mounted on a stand. A row of bullets hung down from the gun and reached into an open box on the ground. The soldier was aiming his weapon right at us, one of his eyes peering intently through his gunsight. Sheer fear struck me. I knew that he could decide to start shooting at any moment, and I felt an icy cold spreading inside me and stood completely still, staring back at him in horror. It was as though my life was draining out of me, turning me into a cold statue. He merely looked back through his gunsight. Time stood still.

Then I heard Minn snap the suitcase closed. The soldier's interrogation was over. She took my cold hand and led me onto the streetcar. As I moved, it was like the ice in my body was starting to crack and fall away from me onto the sidewalk. I ascended the stairs to the streetcar, and Minn got us two seats right next to each other. I remember her quietly trying to reassure me by warming up my hands. Even now, many years later, I can still feel shock waves of dread as I recall that cold scene. I know that if they had discovered that I was Jewish, we would have been whisked away. My life, and Minn's, would have been over.

More War, More Fear

In the summer of 1944, the Allied forces launched an aerial pushback against the Nazis in Belgium, and the explosions grew more frequent. One night, I woke up to loud bangs that sounded like thunderclaps inside my bedroom. Minn ran into my room and yanked me out of bed. We both ran downstairs in our nightclothes. Outside the front door, she grabbed my hand and pulled me across the road. As we ran toward the neighbour's farmhouse, I looked up at the night sky. It had been ripped open by fiercely bright, egg-shaped white lights that were hovering above us, emitting a hushed crackling noise. Later, it was explained to me that those bright lights were floodlights, intended to brighten the landscape for Allied bombers so that they could see their targets at night. Flying high above these floating spotlights, the Allied aircraft were not visible from the ground, so they could avoid being targeted by Nazi anti-aircraft guns. There was a rumour that there was a Nazi airstrip hidden behind clusters of tall trees in the forest behind our house. I believed it was true because one day, I saw two large, dark and very noisy airplanes flying low as they took to the sky, one right after the other, emerging from somewhere in those trees.

Minn continued to pull me as we ran across the road, past the farmhouse and into the garden where, among the patches of vegetables, there was a bomb shelter that I had not noticed before. We scurried down some steps that led to an underground structure. I can still remember the distinct scent of freshly dug earth in that shelter. The shelter was entirely underground, with its walls, ceiling and benches made of wooden planks. When the door was closed behind us, one tiny light attached to the shelter's ceiling showed about eight other people already crouching along two benches, facing each other. Minn told me to make no sound; then the light was turned off. We waited. I heard the droning of many airplanes and explosions from their bombs, some so near they shook our shelter. I was afraid of a bomb dropping on us. Minn sitting next to me was comforting to some extent. As time passed, the sounds began to lessen; then they slowly faded and stopped. We waited a while longer. Someone said we could exit, and one by one, we climbed out of the bomb shelter. I was relieved that none of the nearby farm buildings had been bombed.

I had hoped the school would close because the war's noisy explosions were getting worse, but no such luck. One of the nuns at school showed my class a war movie. Maybe they were trying to prepare us for more noises of war that would accompany the Allies as they intensified their attacks against the Nazis. This was the first movie I ever saw. The images on the screen were black and white, grainy, and they shook slightly because of the creaky movie projector. In the movie, soldiers were wearing the same shallow helmets I had seen in my schoolbooks in pictures of British soldiers from World War I. There was footage of soldiers running, shouting, shooting, and there were the loud noises of bombs exploding and buildings burning.

In one scene, there was a figure standing alone on the street between the burning buildings. A close-up showed he was a young boy, about my age. He was out of breath, and his eyes showed fear. In desperation, he shouted for his mother in front of a burning building: "Mama! Mama!" But no mother came out.

At this moment, it suddenly dawned on me — during my busy time in Baudour, with school, church, homework and new friends, I hadn't seen my parents at all. The last time I had seen my parents was at that dinner in Brussels. When school was over that day, I did not play with my friends. Instead, I went directly home. As soon as I walked into the house, I asked Minn: "Where are my parents?" I could tell from her shocked face that my question had startled her. She asked me why I was suddenly asking about my parents. I explained about the war movie at school, about the boy between the burning buildings, about how he was looking for his mother. Minn nodded in understanding. She asked me to come sit with her on the sofa in our living room. We sat together and she seemed to be trying to speak, but no words came out. She quietly put one arm around me, hugged me and began crying softly. Seeing Minn's tears, my intuition told me that I would never see my parents again. I cried too. Our tears and hugs were followed by a long silence. Soon after, I asked if I could visit the tiny stream across the street, where I often played by myself. I would go there when I was upset with school, or when a friend did not want to play with me, or when I had been reprimanded by Minn.

Minn gave me a big hug at the front door and told me to be back for dinner. I crossed the road, entered the walkway toward the farm's vegetable garden, marvelling at how the bomb shelter was camouflaged by the large leaves on the beanstalks that surrounded it. I walked past the garden and past the small farmhouse. A few chickens roamed freely, clucking while picking at their food near a tall haystack. Along a small path in the wild grass beyond the farm and across a wide and open field, I found the tiny stream, trickling with clean water. It was a gentle stream — clear, narrow and shallow, bordered by low tufts of grass that sloped into a large, flat, open field. I found my usual sitting spot on the higher side of the grass where there was a gentle dip forming a natural sitting area. I took off my shoes and put my feet in the cool water, letting its gentleness run over my toes.

Occasionally, I would come here with a friend, and we'd throw a few twigs into the water, imagining them as boats wandering downstream into mighty rivers. But this day, I wanted to just enjoy feeling the cool water trickle over my toes, the late afternoon sun warming me. I did not try to understand why the calmness of the water was slowly able to reduce my sadness about my parents. All I knew was that just as this stream seemed to be constantly flowing, life would go on.

Renewal

In 1945, the Nazi military suffered a crushing defeat. Europe was in shambles. Millions of people from each side, including civilians, had died. Cities had been decimated by bombings. The economies of previously Nazi-occupied nations were in ruins. But the populations that had been occupied by the Nazis erupted in joy.

In Baudour, a festival was organized in the village centre to celebrate the end of the war. There were food booths, where snacks were being prepared and served, free of charge. Minn, smiling widely, was cooking french fries in one of those booths. Church bells were ringing, regardless of the time of day. Local villagers mingled with American, British and Canadian soldiers, and everyone was laughing with joy. Belgian flags with their bold colour blocks of black, yellow and red that had been hidden away were quickly unfurled and popped out of windows and balconies on most buildings. The war was actually over. No more explosions. No more killings. I felt a huge sense of relief.

Prisoners of war were liberated, and Frantz was a free man. He had been transferred from Mons to a prison in Berlin, which had been liberated by the Soviet army. He had lost considerable weight in captivity but was happy to be free and made his way back to Belgium. One morning soon after he returned, the doorbell rang. Minn opened the door. About twenty people, including dignitaries from Baudour's local council, were standing in a semicircle in front of our house. Someone was carrying a Belgian flag. Some of my friends were there as well. The villagers wanted to honour Frantz with a certificate of appreciation. Minn, Frantz and I came outside, and one of the adults made a short speech welcoming Frantz back as a hero. By now it was known that he had been in the resistance fighting the Nazi occupation and had been imprisoned by the Nazis and survived. Two other people stepped forward, expressed their gratitude and gave Frantz a certificate, then bowed toward him. The entire group sang the Belgian national anthem, bowed, then left. When we went back inside, Minn and I were ecstatic that Frantz had been recognized for his bravery. He seemed happy too, as he was quietly smiling.

After the defeat of Nazi Germany, local collaborators who had cooperated with Nazis were mysteriously shot and killed. There were no police investigations into these murders. The husband of one of my babysitters was known to be a collaborator with Nazis. Yet, he knew about my being Jewish and didn't reveal my identity. That is why Frantz sought him out, invited him to the village square and, in front of the church with numerous villagers watching, made a very public display of shaking hands with him, which probably saved his life.

∼

When the war ended, postal services resumed across the Atlantic Ocean. Possibly one of the first letters to cross that ocean in 1945 was sent to Ottawa from Brussels by Minn's father. He wrote to Greta, my mother's sister. My mother had two sisters — Ida Fekete, who had evaded capture by the Nazis and ended up in Australia with her family, and Greta Cohen, who had met her future husband when he was travelling from Eastern Europe to Canada in the 1920s. Their correspondence grew into love letters and then marriage, and she moved to Ottawa to live with him. Before the outbreak of war, Greta had sought asylum for my parents, but they were rejected because of Canada's policy at the time: "none is too many."[1]

---

1 The words famously uttered by a Canadian government official when asked how many Jews should be let into Canada.

The letter was written in French, and Greta arranged for it to be translated into English, and she invited friends and family to her home in Ottawa to hear it being read. By that time, Greta's husband had passed away, and her parents, my maternal grandparents, had also moved to Ottawa. I was later told that the reading of the letter was quite an event. Guests arrived for afternoon tea at her home, and her three children dressed up for the special occasion.

Greta read the letter, which shared that I was alive and well and living with Minn and Frantz. It also explained that my parents, Elsa and Mathias, had been taken to Auschwitz and that their fates were unknown. When Greta finished reading, there were cheers of jubilation followed by animated conversation; at least the young boy had survived. My Ottawa family decided to have me come to Ottawa to live with them as part of their family. After many months of correspondence, they also agreed to sponsor Frantz and Minn's immigration to Canada. That way, Minn and Frantz could continue their relationship with me.

Until 1947, I continued to live in Baudour with Uncle Frantz and Aunt Minn, going to school and developing friendships. I received parcels of clothes from my Ottawa family, including a leather jacket that I really liked. I imagined my trip to Ottawa and that I would be like the character Tintin from the Belgian comic series, who was welcomed in different parts of the world with his white dog and solved mysteries wherever he went.

I was nine years old when I travelled by myself on a plane to New York. I was greeted there by friends of my Ottawa family and was hosted by a welcoming young woman who had a comfortable apartment in Manhattan with a window from which I could see many lights from other very tall buildings and more lights from the car traffic far below. The following morning, this friendly woman took me to the airport and I boarded a plane to Ottawa. During that trip, the flight attendant asked if any of the other passengers spoke French and could sit next to me because I spoke only French. A man named Eugene Kash switched seats and sat next to me to keep me company.

He was an orchestra musician living in Ottawa, and he ended up becoming a good friend of my Ottawa family.

When I arrived at the Ottawa airport, my Canadian family gave me a very warm welcome. A reporter from a local newspaper was there to document the arrival of one of the first orphans from war-torn Europe. A picture taken by the reporter shows three generations of smiling faces standing at the foot of the stairs to the airplane. There is me, a young boy in short pants and a white collared shirt, wearing a pair of round eyeglasses; my grandparents, Julius and Fanny Gerstl; my mother's sister Greta; Greta's sons, Ed and Sid, and her daughter, Erica (Ricky), who understood French and acted as my translator; the friendly passenger, Eugene Kash; and a family friend.

My family was excited and happy to meet me. I was shy. After retrieving my suitcase, we drove to my new home on a tree-lined street: 242 Clemow Avenue. The family gave me a tour of the spacious home, Ricky serving as the guide because of her knowledge of French. I remember being especially interested in the fireplace, which in the winter would burn real wood logs. The tour ended on the third floor, where I would be sleeping. Ed, my oldest cousin, had his bed on the far side of this room, near a large window. My bed was on the opposite side of the room nestled in a cozy nook next to another window. Colourful pennants on a string hung across the length of my bed. I turned to Ricky and asked for a hammer. She did not understand, so I motioned with my closed hand on an imaginary hammer tapping on an imaginary nail. There was a bit of talk among family members, then Ricky nodded to me, went downstairs and came back with a hammer. By this time, I had opened my suitcase and unwrapped a small cross, which I intended to nail to the wall just above my bed.

Seeing the cross, my grandfather screamed his disapproval, yelling in German, the language I had spoken with my parents before the war but no longer understood. His loud voice was countered by other loud voices which argued in favour of letting me hang up the cross. As this argument was raging all around me, I was more puzzled than afraid. Each person had been so very welcoming to me, so I knew the shouting was not about me. I soon realized the cross was the problem. Minn had packed it and had instructed me how to hang it up. She was hoping I would continue to be Catholic.

Sid, my second oldest cousin, told me later that he had argued that I be allowed to put up the cross, that it was not right to block me from doing it. After all, Christianity had been my religion in Belgium, and it had been the way I hid from the Nazis. He argued that to stop me now could give me the impression that I was not welcome. He also told my grandfather that the family could remove the cross later, but only after I got used to my new home.

Gradually, the voices around me quieted down. My family was now nodding, smiling and motioning to me to put up the cross, which I did. In the days that followed, I was given more colourful decorations, felt flags and pennants from different countries, and I was happy to put them up in my sleeping nook. I felt like I was being welcomed into a circus tent, which thrilled me. I don't know if it was a few days, or weeks or months later but, eventually, someone took the cross down, and I hardly noticed that it was gone.

My Re-emerging Jewish Self

I got used to my new home on Ottawa's fashionable Clemow Avenue. I went to school and took English lessons and made new friends. Ricky's French translation was needed less and less as I learned more English, but she remained a friendly bridge to my new family. She and others were able to make room for an additional family member, showing their emerging love for me, which I was glad to reciprocate. Greta told me to call her Aunt Greta, which I did.

The person in my new household who reached out to me in the most active, intense way was my grandmother, the mother of my birth mother. I experienced my grandmother's love as all-encompassing and unconditional. Her eyes shone brightly through those thick eyeglasses of hers, alongside her wide smile — so expressive, warm and constant, yet gentle. I now recognize that her strongly expressed love for me went a huge way toward smoothing my transition to my new home from the violence of war and genocide.

My grandfather was more distant but always kind toward me. He was a dedicated letter writer. He often sat at his desk on the second floor of the house, where he had a sitting room and bedroom he shared with my grandmother. On his desk he had a small typewriter on which he would *clack-clack* with one finger from each hand in quick succession to produce single-spaced type onto thin airmail paper that he would then mail far and wide to family members and friends.

Frantz was offered employment in Halifax, Nova Scotia, as a scientist with Canada's Department of Fisheries. He and Minn moved there from Belgium not long after I arrived in Ottawa. They visited me in Ottawa periodically, and I visited them once, travelling by airplane to Halifax with my cousin Sid.

I was about ten years old when my adoption papers arrived in Ottawa. By then, Greta had told me that my parents had been murdered by the Nazis, but absorbing the information about their untimely death would come in stages. Though I knew that my parents were among the Nazis' murder victims, I continued to hope well into my teens that one day the doorbell would ring, announcing that they were back. For years, I avoided facing what my parents and others had experienced in Nazi captivity. It was just too painful. It was not until I was an adult that I would venture into my inner life to address that pain and the shame that came with it.

One morning, as I sat in the breakfast nook with Greta, she said, "Good news. Your adoption papers have arrived, you're now officially part of our family. You don't have to call me Aunt Greta anymore. You can call me Mum or Mother." I thought about it and felt good with calling her Mum like my new siblings did.

Then Greta said that she would be happy if I wanted to change my last name to Cohen as well. "You don't need to decide now," she said. "You might like to think about it and let me know in a few days."

But I didn't need a few days. I knew that I wanted to keep the name Carniol to honour my parents. When I told Greta that, she paused for a few moments and then agreed. I would keep my parents' last name.

Reflecting on that interaction now, I wonder if she may have been hurt by my not wanting to accept her name, and I marvel at her willingness to give me the choice. It was like she was offering me a gift that I was turning down, but she was so gracious in accepting my decision that her feelings about it were never discussed. I only grew to appreciate my adoptive mother's wisdom as I grew older.

As I adapted to my new home, I felt my family's respect for my process. They did not pressure me to identify as Jewish again, and instead of talking about Judaism, we lived it. My family welcomed Shabbat, the Sabbath, with blessings over candles that were lit at sundown, everyone at home together for most Friday dinners. We celebrated Jewish holidays together, often with song, as when we lit the Hanukkah candles and sang Hanukkah songs together.

My favourite holiday became Passover, with its traditional dinner, matzah, tasty foods and lively songs. At the seder, my grandfather sat at the head of the table. He would rise and sing a blessing in Hebrew over the wine to indicate the beginning of our seder. I felt awe for the ritual retelling of how God sent plagues to free us from slavery to a tyrant. There were good-natured suggestions by everyone about what the next ritual should be and discussion about the Haggadah, the text that told the story of Passover and served as a guide for the seder.

Then there would be a scrumptious meal of gefilte fish, chicken soup, roasted chicken, tasty potatoes and vegetables, followed by a dessert of fresh fruits. Throughout the seder, we drank at least the four ritual cups of wine, and we ended with songs and the prayer giving thanks to God for the food. I was happy to be included in all these traditions. After the seders, we would go for walks and my family would explain the reasons for the different rituals and answer any other questions I had.

The transition back to my Jewish roots did include some bumps. When that first Rosh Hashanah arrived, my first Jewish New Year in Ottawa, my family was getting dressed up to go to synagogue. Ed, who at times was like a father to me because he was the eldest of my new siblings, asked me: Did I want to come with them, or did I want to stay home? As I was thinking about it, Ed said that he wanted to show me something and pointed to a small blue velvet bag. He explained that inside the bag was a tallis, a prayer shawl that men wear when they're in synagogue. He took the tallis out of the bag, unfolded it and put it over his shoulders. It looked like a large, wide scarf, white, with dark blue stripes along its length. Ed told me that

Sid had one too and that when I got older, I could have one as well. "If you decide to come to the synagogue with us," he said, "and if you want to leave, just take one end of this tallis and pull on it once, and we will both leave right away."

Ed and I had a good rapport, and I trusted him, so I agreed to go to the synagogue with the family. I put on my "Sunday best" clothes and went with Ed. Inside the synagogue, there were hundreds of people already seated, holding prayer books — men were on the main floor of the sanctuary and women on the balcony on the second floor. I was used to the solemnity of a Catholic Mass, where all congregants are silent except for scripted readings. Here, in the synagogue, though the worship service was in full flow, most of the men were talking with each other, and I could hear the low buzzing sound of many voices.

I followed Ed and Sid to their seats toward the front of the sanctuary. They each put on a tallis and sat down. I sat next to Ed and looked up at the women's balcony and was glad when I noticed that Mum and Ricky were waving at me. I waved back. The buzzing sound of men talking around me was quietening down. The cantor began chanting softly. I did not expect what happened next. The cantor took a deep breath, and then gave one loud burst of a call, as if his voice was prying open the gates of heaven to hear his plea.

I was shocked and frightened and did not hesitate; I grabbed one side of Ed's tallis and yanked hard. Poor Ed! He probably did not expect that force. He definitely got my message. Without a word, he got up, took off his tallis, took my hand and led me out of the synagogue. I sensed he had wanted to stay, but he left. My trust deepened because I saw that when Ed made a promise to me, he kept it.

Later, I went to a smaller synagogue, which we called a shul, closer to where we lived. I would go there regularly with my grandparents who could easily walk to it. I learned to no longer fear loud chants from the cantor. There were usually about fifteen members at the shul, with my grandmother often being the only woman sitting in the balcony. My grandparents were treated like honoured guests. My grandfather and the other men would sometimes pass a snuff box around, and as a special treat, they would teach me how to take a pinch of its tobacco and insert it into one of my nostrils. While I sneezed a lot at first, everyone coached me how to do it, until I could snuff without sneezing, while my grandfather's kind face smiled and nodded his approval.

That synagogue also held after-school Hebrew classes that we called cheder. I enjoyed making friends with kids in my Hebrew school. If I got there early, I would enter through the synagogue and go to the basement to play. I had fun playing hide-and-seek with my new friends in that basement with its numerous nooks and crannies.

I continued to go to shul with my grandparents almost every Shabbat. Though I preferred to sleep in on Saturday morning, my grandmother would stand at the bottom of the steps to the third floor and call to me: "Benny, it's time to wake up, time to get washed, time to get dressed, time to come with us to shul!" At first, I would pretend not to hear her, but her gentle voice persisted until she had wakened me enough and I could not go back to sleep.

My grandparents showed such love in the kind way they spoke with me in German, the language they knew best, until I was able to reply in German. They would patiently teach me new German words, and I became fluent enough to speak with them in German. Because of how quickly I was able to speak German with my grandparents, the rest of the family concluded that my parents had spoken German to me at home.

Periodically, Frantz and Minn would visit Ottawa from Halifax. On one of their first visits, when I was about eleven, Minn accompanied me to my bedroom to say goodnight after we finished dinner. When we were alone, she pulled out the cross she wore on her necklace, asking if I still believed in Jesus.

I loved Minn and did not want to hurt her feelings, but I did not want to lie. I decided to tell Minn a story that came to me, about a large tree — it had one of its branches cut, and that branch fell to the ground. That branch was me, I told Minn. And that branch wanted to be reunited with the tree. And that's what happened; the branch was picked up and tied tightly to the tree, and it started to grow new leaves and became part of the tree again. When I finished my story, we were both were quiet. Minn nodded. Her eyes were not angry, just sad. She hugged me, and we said goodnight. She left the room and went back downstairs.

The next morning, when I was having breakfast with my family, someone asked me what Minn had said to me the night before. I told them what happened. They all became furious at Minn. But for me, there was no issue. Minn was Catholic before she knew me. She was still Catholic. I was Jewish before I knew her, then became Catholic for a few years, and now I was Jewish again. It's what I thought, but I'm not sure what I said at that breakfast. One thing I do remember clearly. Ricky came over to me, gave me a big hug and said, "Good for you, Ben. We're proud of you!"

∼

My after-school Hebrew teacher also became my bar mitzvah teacher. He was a gentle person who emphasized developing an interpersonal rapport with students to motivate them to practise and put in the effort required to learn the chants for reading the Torah. The key was to start learning the specific sections of the service well in advance of the bar mitzvah. I had many chances to practise because my shul encouraged youngsters like me to lead parts of the service. In addition, I had the encouragement and approval of my grandparents who were an appreciative audience whenever I participated at shul.

At the age of thirteen, I had a bar mitzvah and made the whole family proud, as well as their friends and many community members. The shul, including the balcony, was packed. I chanted in Hebrew and led much of the Shabbat morning service. I remember my grandfather standing with me on the *bimah* at the front of the shul as we took the Torah out from its cabinet. Then, with my grandfather standing next to me, I sang the traditional chant in a loud and clear voice. When I finished, I glanced at him and saw a very happy, proud grandfather.

Then it was time for me to deliver a short speech that Mum had helped me write. She had asked if I was okay to include one sentence about missing my parents and being sad that they could not attend my bar mitzvah. I agreed and said that I also wanted to make people laugh. I wanted people to know the huge relief I would feel after completing the Torah reading. I added the sound of a big sigh, "WHIEWOO!" which did make people laugh. Ricky later told me that I was a natural speaker, that people cried when I mentioned my parents but were laughing the next minute. Her support meant so much to me.

Responding to Grief

I was not the only one affected by the Nazis' murder of my parents. My adoptive mother grieved for the loss of her sister, and my new siblings grieved as well. My grandparents were grieving the loss of their child. In the evenings, as I did my high school homework at a desk in my bedroom, I would hear my grandfather making sad noises from his and my grandmother's room on the floor below. He would let out a series of sighs, combined with moans. Sometimes there were words in German and sometimes in Hungarian, his first language. At other times he would call out people's names, including the name of his daughter, my mother, Elsa, followed by sobbing noises that gradually grew softer as he fell asleep. This would last ten or fifteen minutes. I felt that if those noises helped him fall asleep then he needed to do it. It became a routine in the evening that we all accepted.

But one evening, instead of sighing and moaning softly, he was shouting louder and louder. I stopped my homework, and when I came down to the second floor, I was surprised to see all my siblings present, along with my adoptive mother and my grandmother. They were all crowded into his bedroom, the overhead light on.

Because of my relationship with my grandfather, at that moment I was able to see his bedroom through his own eyes, and I felt I knew one of the causes of his upset. My grandmother had become a hoarder, though we did not use that term then. There were piles upon piles of newspapers on their beds. My grandmother had left a small space on her bed for her to sleep in and a space for my grandfather on his bed. But every other surface was piled high with newspapers. I knew that my grandfather was neat. On his corner of the desk in their other room, the letters awaiting his reply were stacked in a tidy pile inside a small box. I knew that he had left a successful store that he owned in Czechoslovakia and a home where, like other men at the time, he had probably acted like the master. Since moving to Canada, his world had shrunk to these two small rooms, and he was now being crowded out of his bed by tall stacks of newspapers that my grandmother saved in case she wanted to read them again.

I also thought that maybe, in addition to losing my mother, he had learned about the hundreds of thousands of Jews in Hungary who had been rounded up by the Nazis and sent to death camps and into poison gas chambers where they were murdered. Perhaps he had learned about victims from the part of Hungary he was from.

I knew I had to act quickly. Surprising myself with my certainty, I told everyone that they needed to leave the bedroom. I then asked for someone to bring me a facecloth soaked in cool water, and Ricky quickly got it for me. All the while, my grandfather was screaming hysterically. I turned off the light on his night table, and once everyone had left the room, I turned off the overhead light, closed the door and walked toward my grandfather in the dark. I sat next to him and starting throwing the piles of newspapers off the bed.

Then I talked softly to him, saying in German that I had a cool cloth that I wanted to put on his forehead — was he okay with that? He agreed, and I placed the facecloth on his forehead, stroking his forehead slowly, still talking softly to him. He stopped shouting so that he could hear what I was saying. I said that I loved him, that he should try to get some sleep, that I wanted all the newspapers off both beds, and I would talk to my grandmother about that, but that could only happen tomorrow; now he needed some sleep.

My grandfather whimpered. He loved me too, he said, and was very proud of me. I kept talking to him softly as he calmed down, and he seemed to agree that he needed to sleep. I said I would not leave him until he fell asleep, that I didn't mind how long I needed to wait because I liked his company. His sense of humour was returning, and he challenged me. Did I still love him even if he was just a silly old man? And I said, yes, even if he was just a silly old man. We both chuckled, and soon after, he fell asleep. I waited next to him until I was sure he was sleeping.

When I opened the door, the whole family was in the hallway, listening. We moved down the hall to talk, and Ricky told me that no one else could have calmed him down like that. I explained that for Grosspapa (what I called him in German) it was important that all newspapers stay off both beds and that Grossmama would need to find another place to keep them. Everyone agreed. Even my grandmother agreed because she wanted to avoid a repeat of this evening. Though at the time, I did not have the words to explain what had happened, I did sense that my empathy with his needs had gone on high alert and guided my response.

Echoes of Antisemitism

When I was about twelve years old, I was playing with a group of neighbourhood kids on my street in Ottawa, when out of the blue, one of those kids called me "dirty Jew." I was hurt and became hostile to him. He reciprocated by trying to wrestle me to the ground. He was taller than I was, and he reached over me to grab my arms while trying to pull me down to the sidewalk. I resisted and tried to free myself from his grip, swinging my arms sideways: that didn't work. Then with both my fists clenched tight, I rapidly punched high over my head. I could not see where my punches were landing because he was still behind me and trying to use his weight to pull me down. I kept punching high over my head until I heard *crunch* — followed by his scream. He immediately let go of me. I turned to face him and realized I had landed a lucky punch squarely on his nose. Blood was oozing from his face and, screaming in pain, he ran home. I wiped some of his blood off my clothes and walked home, feeling good about our fight.

When I came home, I sat down for lunch with Ricky and then heard the doorbell ringing. Ricky went to answer it, with me following. When she opened the door, I saw the neighbourhood kid, his face wiped almost clean, blood still leaking from his nose. Next to the kid was his mother, sternly looking at Ricky, who by now was also seeing the blood on the kid's face.

Ricky asked what had happened, and the kid's mother pointed to me, hissing her hostility like a large aggressive snake, "He did thhhhiissss!" I immediately shouted back, pointing at her son, "He called me a dirty Jew!" Ricky now glared at the kid, who had probably thought that his insult would remain our secret. I saw the kid's face and body wilting in front of his mother. She looked back at her son, shaking her head at him in disapproval. Ricky and I just stood there. The mother composed herself, apologized for bothering us and muttered in a low voice that she would be talking to her son. She turned away from the door, took her son by the hand and led him away from our house.

Ricky closed the front door, smiling at me. "Looks like you showed him!" she almost shouted, fully approving of my lucky punch. Soon after, I heard Ricky on the phone, telling her friends her version of what happened. When her friends saw me, they cheered and encouraged me to keep punching out antisemites. It was a bit embarrassing, but I must confess, I did enjoy the way Ricky treated me like a winner, telling her friends about how I had beat up an antisemitic bully twice my size.

In my last year of high school, I had another experience of antisemitism. I was applying to be a carpenter's assistant with the construction company the federal government had contracted to build the Mid-Canada Radar Line at the Great Whale River, near the border between Quebec and Ontario. As part of my application, I was to do a medical check with a doctor in Old Montreal.

The doctor took my blood pressure and listened to my heart. He was an elderly gentleman and personable. He chatted about his practice and asked me which subjects I enjoyed studying. He asked me to do twenty push-ups, and I dropped to the floor and happily showed that I could do those push-ups in quick succession. He said, "It's a joy to see your energy and your cooperation. It's such a contrast from the Jews who come here and act as if they own the place and are terribly sloppy in their push-ups."

I was shocked but did everything I could to hide my feelings and kept smiling while continuing the conversation. I needed him to fill out and sign the medical form so that I could get this job. I steered the conversation away from Jews, and we talked about other things. As the exam was coming to an end, I thanked him for his friendly approach and said with a wink that I hoped I had passed the test. He smiled, saying, "You passed it with flying colours, young man."

At the doorway, as I was leaving, I said, "One more thing: I want you to know, I'm Jewish." His jaw dropped. I quickly shut the door, ran to the elevator, hopped in and headed out to the street. I realized he could try to block my being hired, but I felt he was unlikely to do it because I had a signed copy of his glowing recommendation. And I didn't think he'd want me to complain and bring to light the low-key antisemitism he seemed to be enjoying under the radar.

Awakenings

When I applied to law school, my Ottawa family and friends were pleased. I felt supported by a prevailing narrative that praised my becoming a lawyer, which promised financial rewards, prestige and personal autonomy. After starting at the University of Toronto's law school, I sensed that our professors also wanted us to be successful. They were strict in their demands that we develop high standards for dissecting legal arguments. Most of the students in my class were less subtle about their goals. In one way or another, it became obvious that they wanted not only to become rich, but very rich. In some way, I too shared those ambitions. Yet there was another side of me that wanted to see my future through a different lens.

In high school and university, I had started learning about the various political upheavals during the twentieth century that had serious consequences for people's lives. I had learned that in many parts of the world people lived in conditions of extreme poverty, existing side by side with small pockets of people who were extremely wealthy. I began reading books and articles that linked poverty to various hardships, ranging from malnutrition to shorter life spans. These social issues were increasingly capturing my attention. When I would voice my concerns about what was being done to address poverty and other issues, I sensed that these questions were not particularly welcome among my family members and friends. Nevertheless, I kept thinking about these issues with a quiet tenacity that was not visible under what most people saw as my easygoing disposition.

I can now see that my questions about poverty and wealth reached a critical flashpoint during my first year at law school in Toronto. This was partly due to my exposure to Jewish thought in local synagogues. On as many Saturday mornings as my studies would allow, I would dress somewhat formally in a white shirt, necktie and jacket, and I would visit one of the synagogues located along Lawrence Avenue or those on Bathurst Street, south of Eglinton Avenue. I could easily reach these locations by walking from my basement apartment. I rarely went to the same synagogue twice in a row.

The Jewish education that I had received in Ottawa, supplemented by my family's Jewish practices at home, was strong enough that I was familiar with various Jewish denominations. Sometimes I went to a small Orthodox congregation in a one-room storefront where men, dressed in dark suits and black hats, would sit on hard wooden benches or on rickety folding chairs. They were friendly, making room for me to join them and offering me their prayer books while they took another one for themselves from nearby shelves.

The next time, I would try a large established congregation, either Conservative or Reform, in a spacious, palatial sanctuary with tall, colourful stained-glass windows, where the seats were so soft, I could sink into them and daydream to my heart's content. In the larger synagogues, the prayer leader tended to be more of a performer of cantorial music than in the smaller congregations, where one of the congregants would lead the rest of us in worship. But regardless of the differences, I felt at home in each place, and I looked forward to when the rabbi or spiritual leader would give their talk, or *d'var*, about the Torah reading for that week.

Despite the differences among the various denominations, I found that many of the ideas expressed in these talks overlapped into a series of main messages that called out to me: "Justice, justice shall you pursue ... work for peace ... be kind in your dealings with others ... study Torah to understand God's expectations and instructions to our community ... act ethically in your business, your home, your community ... beware of and protect our people from antisemitism ... support Israel because that too is our home and refuge."

These messages were not new. They reflected the values I had learned from my adoptive family, from my after-school Hebrew classes and from the Jewish culture around me. For my family, these values were important, but they seemed more like background music. By contrast, I increasingly wanted to put these values at the forefront of my life.

During my first year at law school, an unexpected event took me totally by surprise. I was by myself in the sparsely furnished, dim basement apartment that I shared with another student. As a slow reader, I had to spend extra time reviewing my notes and doing the assigned readings for the next class. I was alone in the apartment, reading my notes that were spread out on the table, when suddenly a fierce shaking came over me, like an earthquake. It felt like something was coming loose inside my body, like someone had grabbed me from behind and was shaking me to the core. I turned around, but no one else was there. As my mind raced to try to find the source of this shaking, I tracked it to the lower part of my chest. It felt like a volcano was surging up from deep inside me. I was bewildered and frightened. And then the sensation started to ease off until it stopped entirely. The entire episode lasted for no more than one or two minutes.

I was confused and disoriented. I was still sitting in my chair, and everything seemed the same — the room, my notes spread on the table. In the days and weeks that followed, I tried to make sense of what had happened, but I told no one about my experience.

Now, many decades later, it is evident to me that the shaking was caused by a mixture of personal, emotional and social dynamics that had been percolating deep inside my being; I was releasing several layers of repressed emotion. At the deepest level, I had pushed away my grief for the loss of my parents. Though I had periodically asked Mum and my siblings more about what had happened to them, I quickly learned not to ask. My natural curiosity met with my Ottawa family's need to avoid the topic. I now understand that my family wanted to protect me from the pain of knowing the gruesome details about my parents' murder at the hands of the Nazis. I also believe they were trying to shield themselves from their own pain and the knowledge of what had happened not only to my parents but also to so many others. Perhaps they also experienced tension at some awkward questions: What more could they have done to try to save my parents? Could they have done anything else to have prevented the genocide?

I had also repressed my feelings of gratitude to my rescuers. I had no opportunity to process my shift from being Jewish to being Catholic, then back to being Jewish again. I didn't have a way to process my relocation from Brussels, to Baudour, then to Ottawa, and to now being a student in Toronto. Then, there was a more immediate, niggling question: What did I want to do with my life?

Today I understand the shaking episode partly as my coming out of a cocoon. I had been nudged in a direction that would please my family and fit into what others expected of me, and I fit tightly into that role. During those years, my family members were probably not aware that I felt blocked from finding my own voice and my own direction. I'm not even sure how conscious I was of feeling blocked. After all, I was doing well in my studies, though I had to work hard at them. I had a good social life and enjoyed light romances with some women I was meeting.

Occasionally, I did catch a glimpse of how little choice I had in finding my own path. I knew that the members of my family were good people. They were kind to me, they cared about me and they wanted the best for me. In turn, I cared about them. And so, for a long time I went along with their opinions and their choices because I felt they knew what was best for my well-being. Yet, deep down, their prescription for my happiness left me feeling empty. I began asking myself more frequently: Where could I find a meaningful direction in my life?

To cope with the heavy demands of the law school courses, I developed intensive study habits. I was treading water, which worked well enough, but what was pulling me down were questions I had about the law itself. Those questions began in my first year of law school, when I had no time to process them because of the high volume of coursework. Yet the questions continued to trouble me during my second year of law school, becoming more pronounced with each additional course.

I could not articulate this then, but at an intuitive level, I recognized that the law and its interpretations had built-in biases. The law favoured landlords over tenants. It favoured workplace managers over employees. It put a stronger emphasis on property rights than on human rights. I questioned the prevailing assumption that everyone had equal access to justice. I noticed that the more money you had, the more you could pay a group of lawyers to develop a strong case with better legal strategies, the stronger the odds were of winning your case, even if you had a weak case to begin with. I saw a gap between fairness and legal doctrines, and that gap was souring my view of the law.

All these questions tapped into that part of my inner life that was slowly becoming more focused on social justice. I was learning that poverty was a scourge, present not only in poor nations but also in Canada. I became impatient that my law courses were not dealing with such issues.

My inner voice was becoming louder. It was telling me: "Change direction! Find a path that gives more meaning to your life!" When I started searching for a new direction, I told my family that I was reassessing whether I wanted to become a lawyer. They all advised me to first finish my law degree and then choose whether to practise law or do something else. At the time, I did not recognize how privileged I was to have their financial support. Because of that support, I was able to complete all my courses for the law degree. But my heart was not in it.

As I was completing my law courses, I stumbled on a profession that I knew nothing about: social work. Driven by curiosity, I tracked down a couple of social workers and asked them if I could meet for an information interview. They were happy to meet with me, and I went to their offices. Both social workers impressed me because they talked about their work as alleviating the stress experienced by their clients. They told me about the body of knowledge based on social science research that guided their work and about the importance of developing trusting and empathic relationships with clients to encourage confidence. Their approach was so different from the ways courts worked — in litigation, the emphasis was on winning — and the more I learned about social work, the more I liked it.

My family was not thrilled when I announced that I wanted to become a social worker. I distinctly remember my mother frowning in stern disapproval, verging on disgust. Yet to her credit, when she realized how serious I was about my new direction, she relented. She and my siblings agreed to my proposal that I would continue finding employment during summers. My earnings from summer jobs would pay for my tuition and course textbooks. My family would pay for my food and rent for a small room while I studied for my social work degree from McGill University in Montreal.

So off I went in a brand-new direction, having little sense of where I would end up, yet feeling confident that social work was a better fit for me. I found my courses in social work more meaningful than my law courses because they focused on empathy and on listening to and caring about others.

Quest for Meaning

As many stories about the Holocaust gradually became a matter of public record in the 1950s and 1960s, I began to realize that I was part of a community that had a long history of being despised. I started to think more about societal prejudices and became curious about why people who were considered different were vulnerable to discrimination. Was it because they were different, or was it because the tormentors felt they could escape punishment? I realized that in wartime, it was easier to kill the enemy when the enemy was portrayed as less than human. I began to understand that Nazi thinking, and fascist thinking in general, involves scapegoating innocent people, which leads to genocide.

Accounts by witnesses like Anne Frank and Elie Wiesel, as well as by non-Jews like Corrie ten Boom from the Netherlands, and many other survivors who are not as well known, were documenting the injustices and cruelty caused by racist prejudices. Autobiographies and memoirs were being published, and testimonies made their way into Holocaust museums, archives, history textbooks and, later, onto online platforms. These accounts were studied by researchers, scholars and writers, and provided the backbone for public education about Nazi atrocities.

For years, I avoided facing what my parents and others had experienced under Nazi rule. Partly, I had internalized the feeling that somehow we Jews had done something wrong. Some Jews responded to persecution by deciding to no longer identify as Jewish. After all, it had been dangerous to do so. But I was curious about my Jewish identity. I felt I owed it to my parents to at least try to understand what the accusations were against Jews.

I learned that the Catholic Church taught that Jesus was Jewish but that it also viewed Jews as being responsible for killing him. That myth goes back over two thousand years and set in motion concerted attacks against Jews throughout history. I learned that Christianity became a powerful empire and that its large array of priests, monks and papal officials used their near monopoly of the new printing press to vilify Jews. Their wrath was also unleashed against followers of Islam: several Christian Crusades during the eleventh to thirteenth centuries mobilized thousands of Christians who moved across Europe to attack Muslims who controlled Jerusalem and the surrounding areas. While these militarized pilgrims marched through Europe, they entered Jewish communities and torched them, a practice-run for the subsequent centuries of pogroms, terror and slaughter of countless Jews.

A widespread hatred of Jews was magnified by Christians leaders throughout history. The sixteenth-century theologian Martin Luther, for example, advocated burning synagogues, expulsions and killing Jews. It became clear to me that, given the pervasive Jew-hatred already established, once Nazi Germany invaded other European nations, it would have been easy for local officials to use their positions of authority to further spread the poison of hate against my community.

As I grew in my understanding of the assault against Jews throughout history, I learned that my parents' names were on a list, like the names of other Jews in Belgium and other countries occupied by the Nazis. These lists became an essential part of the Nazis' plan to send Jews to the camps. As I began to learn about Nazi concentration camps, I began to think that "factories of murder" was a more accurate designation because murder was the intent and the result of those Nazi prisons from hell.

There was one question I heard repeated that still haunted me: Why did Jews in Nazi Europe go to their deaths like sheep to the slaughter? While there were some examples of Jews arming themselves and using guerrilla tactics to attack the Nazi war machine, the majority did not take up arms. For years, that question upset me because I felt it wrongly accused my parents and so many other victims of being naive, or of having no courage. Gradually, I came to recognize that this form of blaming the victim revealed a shameful ignorance about the disempowerment experienced by Jews who had been singled out and stripped of their legal, economic, religious and human rights. Under those slavery-like circumstances, with loaded guns pointed at them, if Jews had resisted arrest, transportation and incarceration, they would have been shot on the spot. And many were. Some choice! Worst of all, such negative judgment against victims displayed a shocking failure of compassion toward people whose capacity to defend themselves had been severed by the Nazi apparatus of genocide. As the years passed, I rebelled against that question because I sensed that behind it there was contempt for the victims. I wanted to express compassion for everyone who had been rounded up and forced to experience the horrors of Nazi brutality. Yet, although I could express deep empathy for those who had suffered, it took me much longer to develop feelings of compassion toward myself.

There is no question that survivors of genocide, war and violent abuse carry heavy burdens: trauma, anger, frustration and shame. Sadly, such emotional wounds can lead to bitterness, hatred and various forms of self-destruction. I was fortunate to be supported along a different path, a more constructive one, where healing became possible. It was a path that allowed me to ask: What must be done to block the violence of power abuses, to prevent the massive pain of war and genocide? I was able to ask such questions only after I had rejoined my family and embraced my Jewish identity again.

Community Activism

After graduating with a social work degree, I searched job ads in social work journals and found that in Cleveland, Ohio, social agencies were hiring neighbourhood workers to do community development. I applied and was offered a job there in 1964.

My favourite subjects while training as a social worker were community work and policy analysis. I was attracted to these subjects because I felt they offered the best frameworks for organizing at a grassroots level in partnership with community members. My new position in Cleveland was at Alta House, a community centre in a low-income neighbourhood where most residents were of Italian ancestry. I was hopeful that my studies had prepared me to work on a community level and identify which policy changes would be most appreciated by the local residents.

Soon after I started my job, I moved into the neighbourhood where I was employed, Little Italy. I rented the second floor of a very small house on a quiet side street. My boss, Al Alissi, was a seasoned social worker. He had considerable credibility in the neighbourhood because he would go camping with youth who were at times in conflict with the police. They would have a great outdoor experience, and he would influence them to move away from a life of crime.[1]

---

1 Al Alissi died in 2007. A beautiful tribute published in the *Hartford Courant*, August 23, 2007, offered a glimpse into his caring values.

Al mentored me on how to do social work counselling with neighbourhood residents. He also gave me good advice on how to accomplish my main task in my new role, which was to organize a new neighbourhood council made up of community members. Al consulted some local leaders about who should be invited to this new council. Members of the new council included a Cleveland city councillor whose district encompassed our area and who was a strong advocate for enforcing housing codes. The council also included a respected priest who officiated at the Catholic Church that towered over the centre of our neighbourhood; he personally knew members of Cleveland's Italian community and also some of the landlords. Another council member owned a grocery store in the area and another had been a successful boxer in his earlier years and was now a boxing coach. I later learned that a member of our council was rumoured to be well connected with organized crime.

We met for the first time in the boardroom of Alta House one early evening. The members saw this first meeting as an opportunity to orient me to what they wanted the council to do. I listened, taking some notes. One member after another said they wanted to improve housing and other conditions in their neighbourhood. They identified a number of rental houses that were in disrepair, causing problems for tenants and giving a shabby appearance to the area. Toward the end of the meeting, it was suggested that I take down the addresses of the worst offenders and track down the absentee landlords. I agreed to contact them and try to get them to do the needed repairs.

After the meeting, I tracked down the landlords and phoned them. Their responses ranged from indifference to hostility. I was disappointed, and I wondered if I wasn't doing my job well enough. When the council met for the second meeting, a month later, they were also disappointed with the results. The council agreed that the absentee landlords must be made more accountable. While they had some sympathy for the landlords who did not want to spend money on roofing and plumbing and other repairs, they also felt that the landlords needed to take more responsibility for their neighbourhood and their tenants.

The council decided on a new plan. I would send letters to all the landlords I had contacted, politely requesting that they cooperate by doing the necessary repairs. The letter was signed by all members of the council, and I mailed them out, letting out a sigh of relief when I saw the staff at the post office put the letters in their mailbox.

And lo and behold! We soon saw repair trucks, roofers, painters and other repair people coming to fix the homes that needed it. I felt as though I had a front-row seat in witnessing the power of organized community to take charge where there was a lack of social responsibility. I reported the results at the next council meeting, and the council members gave me an enthusiastic vote of confidence for the efficient implementation of their plan.

I heard similar stories from social workers in other parts of Cleveland. They spoke about community organizers throughout the United States helping tenants to organize themselves and carrying out rent strikes in large apartment blocks, demanding the required repairs. It was a time when community initiatives were gaining strength in many parts of the United States, and there was a sense of optimism that local grassroots organizations could pressure politicians to support their work and make it sustainable. The civil rights movement was gathering steam, and students on university campuses were organizing for changes in the curriculum and were joining protest movements. It was in this environment that I felt the power of my work with our new neighbourhood council.

Even before learning about the results of the letters, I was happy to be working at Alta House. I felt support from each of the council members and from my boss and colleagues as we developed a team approach. I was thrilled to be tackling the housing issue, and the results of our efforts were far better than I had expected. I became confident that the downward slide of housing conditions in the city could be stopped and reversed through organized community action.

Voter Registration

In the 1960s, Cleveland erupted in violence. In 1966, a White bartender in Hough, a Black neighbourhood, refused a Black man a glass of water, which ignited a violent reaction among the Black community in Cleveland. The media was calling these acts of violence "riots," but I saw it differently. I was listening to and learning from Black social workers and their accounts of anti-Black racism experienced by the people they were trying to help. To me, these seemed to be not riots but uprisings by people fed up with being mistreated.

The Black social workers I knew taught me about the existence of vociferous, sinister voices that opposed any assistance to Black Americans. These voices were led by White supremacist groups such as the Ku Klux Klan. I was upset that these White bigots were able to hide their identities behind the White veils of power that for centuries had imposed racial segregation and subjugation. I learned that their violence included cross-burning, lynching, house-burning and murder of White activists who were organizing against anti-Black racism. There were also plenty of racist sheriffs, judges and business leaders who were colluding with, if not leading, the anti-Black racism that permeated American society.

On a daily basis, I heard so much chatter that normalized racism. On the radio I'd hear voices say, "Racism is just part of human nature. It happens everywhere. That's just how people are." Yet my gut told me this was wrong. I would become frustrated when I heard apologists claim that racism was only a minor issue that caused no serious harm. One thing I was certain about: racism against Jews had caused severe harm; it had caused genocide. And anti-Black racism had violently wrenched an estimated 12.5 million Africans from their national homelands, cruelly chained them and forced them to provide free labour for the White owners of plantations in North America and elsewhere. I was also learning about the barbaric anti-Black racism that had historically been perpetrated against Black communities. I felt there were some similarities with Jewish communities experiencing centuries of persecution in Europe. Black and Jewish communities had both endured racial insults, discrimination and violence that had defined them as outsiders and "inferior." I began to learn about Black American culture and read books by Black writers such as James Baldwin and Stokely Carmichael. I learned to appreciate jazz, Black musicians and other Black cultural artists. And I started to identify with those who were challenging anti-Black racism.

In 1967, there was going to be an election for the mayor of Cleveland. I wanted to volunteer to register Black voters, so on a day off from work, I drove to the voter registration centre to be interviewed for a volunteer position. The centre was in a suburb that was new to me, a neighbourhood with many small homes, populated mainly by Black Americans. The interview took place in a small community hall. Several men sat around a table, and I was invited to sit with them. I later learned that these men had strong ties to Martin Luther King, Jr.'s organization, the Southern Christian Leadership Conference.

My interviewers asked me how long I had been in Cleveland, where I was working. They were friendly, and I felt relaxed. They asked me what I knew about their candidate. I knew that Carl Stokes was a Black lawyer who had been elected as a Democrat to the Ohio House of Representatives for three terms and that he supported the civil rights movement and anti-poverty programs. I said that I felt that Stokes was by far the best candidate because of his record of favouring social programs, his attention to improving the economy, and his support of Black communities and women.

I was asked if I would be willing to drive prospective voters over the summer, to shuttle them from their homes to voter registration offices that were run by the city of Cleveland. I told them that I'd be willing to drive, but I had concerns about my safety; since I was visibly White, I might not be welcomed. They said they would come up with a safety plan. But first, they had to get to know me better, so they put me to work at their office, doing filing, carrying supplies, making phone calls and doing other activities under the watchful eyes of one of their main organizers. When he was sufficiently satisfied that I was a responsible person, they put the plan into effect.

The appointed time in June was a bright summer day. I drove to the voter registration office, where I was given the names and addresses of the people I was to pick up. The organizers supplied me with a map and made sure that I understood their driving directions. Then I was introduced to the safety plan. I was to ride with children who had gotten to know me as I did my volunteer work at the office. Two would ride in the front of the car with me, and two would be in the back. Their ages ranged from about eight to thirteen. They were given instructions to accompany me wherever I needed to go that afternoon, and then we all hopped into my car and got set to chauffeur potential voters back and forth. As I drove into the heart of Cleveland's Black neighbourhood, I was never stopped or intimidated. I grew confident that my "bodyguards" — happily talking and laughing — were doing their job.

My first stop was at the home of an elderly Black woman. I was nervous, wanting to do a good job, reminding myself to follow the instructions not to discuss the candidates with her. The woman was elderly and frail, and I offered her my arm for support as she came down the stairs from her home. As we drove to the registration office, she told me that she had wanted to vote for a long time but never got around to it. But her neighbour had told her that they were going to vote in this election, so she decided she would too. She was glad for the car ride, which made it easier for her to register. She spent most of the car ride happily chatting with my young passengers.

When we arrived at the municipal building where voters were being registered, I saw other Black Americans coming to make sure they were on the voter list. We approached the city employee and gave her a stack of papers, including paid bills showing the prospective voter's address and showing dates that indicated that she had lived there quite a while. I said I was hoping those papers were acceptable and that we did not have to go back and get more papers. I wanted that employee to know we would be back if necessary. She gave me a bored look, studied the papers carefully and then gave my companion a piece of paper showing that her name had been added to the voter's list. This event, with minor variations, was repeated over and over for the next three months. I often wondered what was going on in the minds of these silent employees who were registering so many Black American voters.

Although voter registration within the Black community took a lot of work, an impossible dream was blossoming right before our eyes. With the hard work, experience and skill of Black organizers, a transformation was occurring. The organizers at the voter registration centre had expressed concern over the apathy they saw in their community, but among most of the new voters I met there was an emerging excitement about new possibilities and hope for a better future.

I have a vivid memory of the way that Dr. Martin Luther King, Jr.'s organization succeeded in getting people to attend a voter registration rally. As part of my volunteer activity, I had agreed to help announce a rally for Dr. King that was to be held on the next Sunday. I drove behind a truck that had loudspeakers hooked up to it. The truck slowly drove up a residential street lined with small single-storey houses where many Black people lived, music playing at full volume. When they heard the music, people came out of their houses and some sat on their porches to listen. A number of children and teens began dancing to the upbeat rhythm of the music, some following the vehicles as they danced. Periodically, the music would be interrupted by a short announcement giving details about Dr. King's upcoming rally. During the announcements, our two-vehicle convoy would stop, and my passenger and I would hop out of my car to distribute the flyers about the rally. We did this for hours, threading our way through the streets in this residential area. By the time we were finished, most of the residents in the area knew about next Sunday's event.

I had heard Dr. King speak once before at a Cleveland city forum to which social workers and many others were invited. One of his messages to us and to the Black community was "Learn, baby, learn!" I took his message to be that Black people and their supporters needed to keep up the nonviolent marches, rallies and demonstrations. These protests were necessary to remove racist barriers in educational institutions that had relegated Blacks to being second-class citizens within America. I was inspired by King's courage in disagreeing with some forceful voices within his own community that were urging "Burn, baby, burn!" These different approaches may have had the same goal of racial equality, but their methods were worlds apart.

I understood the "Burn, baby, burn!" message of the Black militants to mean that the flames of outrage at racism required violent acts of defiance. I could see that such fiery threats would shatter the stereotypes of Black subservience, but I was drawn to King's message of nonviolence and felt welcomed as an ally in the struggle for a racially inclusive America.

On the day of the Sunday rally, it was sunny and there was a clear blue sky. By the time I got to the park, many people of all ages were already sitting on a grassy slope that was like a natural amphitheatre; others had brought their own folding chairs or blankets. Dr. King was ushered onto a small platform at the base of the slope. I marvelled at how many people were still arriving. As I looked around, it seemed to me that I was the only White person in the entire crowd. I noticed Dr. King looking at me. Then he began to speak about how times were changing, how White people were now joining the movement. He welcomed us "brothers and sisters" and said it was time for all of us to work together to create a better world, where we judge people by the merits of their efforts rather than by the colour of their skin.

Then, King went on to urge people to vote, saying that he wouldn't tell people who to vote for, that it was up to everyone to choose and make their vote count. He urged the crowd to tell neighbours, family members, everyone: get registered before voting day, and then, when the time comes, get out and vote. We have that right, he said, so we should use it to build a better future for everyone.

On November 7, 1967, the vote was held. Carl Stokes won. I was elated. He became the first Black person to be elected mayor in a major Northern city. He was part of a new wave of Black Americans being elected to political office.

I had learned much about voter registration and grassroots organizing, and in that process, I had crossed over the American racial divide. But I realized that much depended on my receiving permission to cross over by people from "the other side." My approach was based on a genuine respect for the Black Americans I met, and over time, I got to know the organizers and volunteers not as the "other" but as individuals who had their aspirations and dreams for a decent life, just like everyone else. As they got to know me as well, we formed relationships based on mutual respect, from which mutual trust evolved.

My involvement in the civil rights movement gave me a sense of meaning and the feeling that my life was on the right track. I was doing something practical toward combatting racism in the United States. Though my contribution was small, the fact that I could participate in a process that resulted in a victory like this — electing a Black mayor in a major city — proved something. "People power" was not just an empty phrase; I was experiencing first-hand how it was possible to help motivate people to become enthusiastic, excited and single-minded in surging forward as a group to achieve social progress.

Worlds Apart: The Vietnam War and Memories of Belgium

As I was engaging in my volunteer activities and in my work at Alta House, I also became interested in world events and specifically in the people of Vietnam who were experiencing bombings and death from violence in a brutal war that was tearing their world apart. Some of my Cleveland colleagues and friends were criticizing the United States military for waging an immoral war in Vietnam. But I had good memories of American soldiers. They had given me chocolate bars when the war ended in Belgium, and they were friendly to people in Baudour. I knew that American soldiers, pilots and sailors had risked their lives to defeat the Nazis in World War II, and I was grateful for their sacrifices. Now American soldiers were again risking their lives in Vietnam, but they were being criticized. I found this confusing.

I saw a notice that someone was going to be speaking about the Vietnam War at Hillel, a Jewish student organization, at a university near me. The event was a small gathering, run like a seminar. I asked the speaker: If the US military is involved in Vietnam to protect democracy, why should we oppose it? The speaker replied that my view is exactly what the Lyndon B. Johnson administration wanted everyone to believe. He pointed out that investigative reporters had found that the US administration was hiding the true story from the American public, and he recommended books and magazine articles that we could read.

I took up his suggestion, and in my spare time, I went to libraries and bookstores, tracking down the articles and books he had recommended. I learned details about how the Cold War was being fought in Southeast Asia, with the United States and its allies on one side and the Soviet Union and China and their allies on the other, each side competing for a larger sphere of influence. I learned about Buddhist monks setting themselves on fire in public, killing themselves to draw attention to the ruthless persecution of Buddhists by South Vietnamese authorities, the very government that the United States was supporting.

As I was trying to make sense of it all, I was having intense conversations with my growing network of friends and colleagues in Cleveland. Some of them went to a rally to demonstrate their opposition to the Vietnam War, and I went with them. Yet I was uneasy. I felt like I was being thrown into one side of a conflict that I was only starting to learn about. While there certainly was camaraderie, friendship and shared excitement about being inside a growing grassroots peace movement, I wondered: Were peace activists being used as pawns to embarrass the United States? What else was going on behind the scenes that we had no knowledge of?

Despite my uncertainties, I was beginning to understand some facts. In 1971, the Pentagon Papers were leaked to the public, showing that the US government was indeed lying to the American people about the Vietnam War. American leaders had told us we were in Vietnam to protect democracy, yet the American government was propping up an undemocratic and autocratic regime in South Vietnam. American officials had told us that the American military role was honourable, yet napalm bombs were being used to burn and kill innocent people in villages. American officials had promised that superior American firepower would soon end the war. Instead, the war dragged on as thousands of American soldiers were killed and many more injured, and a far larger number of Vietnamese people were being killed and injured.

I was beginning to reassess my attitude toward the US military forces. I was still grateful to them and their allies for their role in World War II in defeating the Nazi regime, but based on my research, I concluded that the situation now was very different from the 1940s. The more I read and learned about the war, the more I saw that the US military was trying to impose its will upon the Vietnamese population. And so, despite my initial doubts, I continued to oppose and protest the war.

In the spring of 1968, as I was planning a trip to New York City, where there was going to be a huge anti-war protest march, I received a shock. Martin Luther King, Jr. had been assassinated. Dr. King was one of my heroes. I so admired his courage in leading nonviolent marches and rallies against anti-Black racism and his leadership abilities in being able to inspire so many people. He was eloquent in articulating a future when we would be free of racist discrimination, free of racist laws, policies and practices. He shared his heartfelt dreams and challenged me and the rest of us to move toward them.

Though his assassination shocked me, I was not entirely surprised. In my job, I had heard a lot of street talk, and people were often threatening to kill Dr. King. In one instance, I heard a threat against King that I felt was more than just talk. I phoned the Cleveland police and reported it, but it became clear that the police didn't take my concern seriously. One of Carl Stokes's first actions after he was elected mayor of Cleveland was to fire Cleveland's police chief who had a reputation of being hostile toward Black communities, one of several bold moves by the new mayor.

After King's assassination, I noticed a chill among those of us who were protesting the Vietnam War. Our spirits were subdued, but not enough to stop our protests. A group of us travelled by bus to New York, where we joined a huge peaceful demonstration on Fifth Avenue. I was astonished to see large numbers of people surging into the streets to join the protest. People came from all walks of life. There were men in suits carrying attaché cases; there were parents walking with their children, some pushing baby carriages; and there were customers coming out of stores to join. There were so many people, I could not see the speakers' platform or hear the speeches from the loudspeakers that had been installed along New York's streets. It was exhilarating for me to be with so many others in nonviolent protest.

At one point during the march, we came upon a small group of about a dozen neo-Nazis, each one carrying a flag with a large black swastika on it. They were marching in a circle, waving their flags, shouting insults at us. I was both scared and outraged. Before we knew it, New York City police officers swooped in and muscled their way between us and the neo-Nazis. Other officers brought in portable street barriers, which they quickly put around the neo-Nazis, preventing them from moving outside their small circle. It also prevented the rest of us from rushing into that hateful circle and triggering the violent confrontation that the neo-Nazis probably hoped would distract from the message of our march. As I marched on and looked back, it felt good to see the neo-Nazis being lost in a huge crowd of protesters that were continuing to swell through the streets.

After returning to Cleveland, I was keen to read what its main newspaper, *The Plain Dealer*, would say about what I had witnessed. The newspaper's coverage was disappointing and insulting. Prominently displayed in its coverage of the protest was a photograph of a youth with long, wild, unkempt hair, rows of beads around his neck, his eyes slightly unfocused. He seemed to be on drugs. The Cleveland paper had succeeded in mocking and distorting the entire event, and I resented its misrepresentation of what had been a peaceful and well-organized protest that drew thousands upon thousands of people.

Despite such dishonesty in the media, I also witnessed the tide of public opinion turning. Opposition to the role of the United States in the Vietnam War was gathering steam not only on American campuses, but also in many parts of the world. The media that had buried stories about the war sensed the public mood changing and belatedly adjusted its approach to present a more balanced picture of what was happening.

While the US military continued to pursue its war, there was also a steady shift in public opinion. The grassroots efforts of local anti-war networks formed a viable, nonviolent social movement that eventually stopped the leaders of one of the most powerful nations from imposing their will on another nation. At the same time, pundits on the radio and TV tried to exonerate the United States' role in Vietnam by saying that, anyway, aggression and wars were inevitable; they were just part of human nature. But my inner life rebelled against what I was hearing. How did they know that aggression was inevitable? How did they know that wars were predetermined by human nature?

Those were turbulent times and they had an impact on my thoughts and feelings, which I refer to as my inner life. My experiences since arriving in Cleveland had caused me to question assumptions I had about the United States. I had believed it to be a fair country, a land of equal opportunity. But what I was learning about anti-Black racism and the civil rights movement punched a hole in that belief, bringing me face-to-face with pervasive poverty and racism. I had also believed that the United States was leading the fight against oppressive regimes around the world; now I was learning that the United States had invaded Vietnam and destroyed its villages because of fear of communist influence. All this left me confused, wondering which of my other beliefs needed adjustment. Yet I felt that my new understandings, though uncomfortable, were less naive and much closer to reality.

Meanwhile, Al Alissi left Alta House: he had been hired by the School of Social Work at the University of Connecticut. My colleagues and I congratulated him while I suppressed my sense of feeling abandoned. After all, it was normal to move on. Moving every few years was expected of professionals who were climbing their career ladder. Soon afterwards, I was the one to do the abandoning of my friends, co-activists, work colleagues, neighbours and our neighbourhood council when I resigned from Alta House and left Cleveland in order to seek new professional opportunities. The president of Alta House's board of directors wrote me a warm, heartfelt letter of appreciation for my having worked diligently with leaders in Little Italy to successfully reverse the neighbourhood's housing deterioration, which helped counteract the small twinge of guilt I experienced at leaving.

Jim Chang, a good friend from my days as a social work student at McGill University, suggested I return to Montreal because he knew there were jobs available for social workers there. I took his advice and applied to the Montreal Council of Social Agencies, a social development agency that gathered recommendations from social workers and their clients about what social service priorities should be funded by government, private foundations and other funding organizations. I was hired, and in 1969 returned to Montreal.

As I moved back to Canada, I was aware that my inner life had been affected by my experiences in Cleveland, which would shape my life as I continued to search for justice. I had learned to trust what I was hearing from clients and their advocates. I had learned that systemic racism was denied by narratives of conventional wisdom and glib comments about human nature justifying prejudices and injustices that were harming so many people. When the Kerner Commission's report[1] validated my conclusions about racism in America, I felt I needed to trust myself more. I learned that as I was helping to empower others, I was also empowering myself. I was grateful that I had switched to social work and was now learning first-hand about injustices that needed to be challenged on the road to social progress.

---

1 A report commissioned by the Johnson administration to inquire into the cause of rioting in the United States. Issued in 1968, it concluded that rioting was caused by frustration at lack of economic opportunities.

Anti-Poverty Activism

My work at the Montreal Council of Social Agencies involved listening to social workers and their clients as they expressed frustration at what they felt were the punitive attitudes of government welfare offices. Welfare cheques paid amounts so low that recipients could not afford enough food to live on. We would hold meetings for welfare clients and social workers. About twenty-five of us would gather in a community centre, sitting in clusters for specific neighbourhoods. There was a sense of enthusiasm because participants saw we were listening. My inner life realized that this was the constructive part of social work — being in direct contact with people experiencing poverty and other social issues. We could either say there was nothing we could do, or we could figure out how to respond better to those issues. To do nothing was not an option, so we brainstormed about how to work for change. And that felt good.

We decided to call ourselves the Greater Montreal Anti-Poverty Coordinating Committee, and I was chosen, along with Helen Bastien, a welfare recipient, to be a co-chair of the committee. Helen volunteered to take minutes, and I met with her over tea at her home to review them. Helen told me that she had been employed as a bookkeeper, but when her husband was found guilty of a crime and jailed, her family income was not enough to meet her expenses as a single mother of two young children, so she was receiving welfare. When

I had reviewed Helen's minutes, I was surprised: they were totally accurate. I had accepted the prevailing prejudices against people living in poverty, which devalued their skills and capacities. I started to realize that I was embarking on a new learning curve.

The committee decided to set up information tables in welfare offices to share information with welfare clients about what they were entitled to under the Quebec regulations. But most welfare offices refused to grant us permission. We came up with a plan with help from the Parallel Institute, which was led by Peter Katadotis. He was a visionary social worker who had good connections to the National Film Board, which provided us with the telephone hardware we needed to carry out our plan.

On a designated morning, three members from our anti-poverty committee walked up one flight of stairs to the lobby of a welfare office in Montreal. There, they set up some chairs and a portable table on which they put our information flyers and a pot of hot coffee. They greeted welfare clients coming to the office, offering them information and coffee. A welfare administrator soon appeared and asked the three at the table what they were doing. They replied that they were volunteers who were offering information about the correct rates listed in the government's policies, and they gave her a flyer. The administrator asked that they leave. They declined. She insisted that they leave. They declined. The administrator left in a huff and presumably reported it to her supervisor, who called the police.

Meanwhile, another committee member and I were waiting in a parked car near the entrance to the welfare office. We had an old-fashioned battery-operated walkie-talkie system and used it to speak with our three friends inside the welfare office. Within about half an hour, we heard sirens in the distance, slowly growing louder. When we saw a group of police officers on motorcycles, wearing black uniforms and white helmets, riding into view, we radioed to our friends inside and told them it was time to pack up. They folded the table and chairs, packed the coffee urn and walkie-talkies, and started down the stairs. The police had parked their motorcycles and entered the building. As they went up the stairs, they met three harmless looking, neatly dressed people coming down the stairs. The last police officer in the group held the door open for our friends as they left the building. Our friends quickly put their things into our car and jumped in. When they closed the car door, we all burst out laughing as our driver hit the gas pedal to speed away in our "getaway car" so that we could repeat the performance at another welfare office. We were reminded that activism could also be fun.

The committee was busy. We demonstrated in front of a Montreal hospital to protest the runaround and lack of hospital service that had been the experience of welfare clients. We held sit-ins at a welfare office to protest the inadequate rates of welfare payments until the police evicted us. We made deputations to Quebec's ministry in charge of welfare and were even given a police motorcycle escort as we approached Quebec City. Nevertheless, many of us felt that something was amiss. Despite the media attention that we gained, Montreal's welfare rates were still far below the poverty level. We had sent briefs to heads of government. We had talked with journalists and with documentary filmmakers. We had held public meetings and conferences. We had met with public officials. All these activities had kept us very busy, yet we were preoccupied by the question: Why were we not successful in making more substantial change?

I realized that we were up against laws and long-standing public attitudes that blamed the poor for being poor. But I shared the disappointment of others that, after all our efforts, the welfare rates offered by the Quebec government were not increasing. I felt we were failing to make any real change in the social conditions of Montrealers who were living in poverty.

∼

The mayor of Montreal, Jean Drapeau, led a campaign to bring the 1976 Summer Olympic Games to Montreal, which would require the city of Montreal to commit substantial funds to plan and build the infrastructure for the Games. As anti-poverty activists, we felt that the city should channel more funds to help Montrealers who were struggling with poverty. Mayor Drapeau did not hear us. His single-minded advocacy for these Summer Olympics succeeded when the International Olympic Committee chose Montreal. The elated mayor organized an international press conference to showcase how the Summer Olympics would endear Montreal to the world. On the day of the press conference, some members of the Greater Montreal Anti-Poverty Coordinating Committee learned where and when it would be taking place. We had little chance to prepare. I rushed home to put on a sports jacket then met several activist friends outside a tall downtown office building where the mayor's press conference had been scheduled.

As we entered the main-floor lobby, we saw a long table where people were lining up to show their invitations or press credentials. A cluster of people carrying television equipment passed by us and headed toward the elevators, and I began walking beside this small crowd of media technicians. I looked back and noticed my friends being stopped by security guards. One of the crew was carrying a heavy camera on his shoulder. Though we had never met before, he said to me quietly as we entered the elevator, "You're in. Just come up."

We exited on a higher floor, and I entered a large auditorium with individual desks and chairs in rows and a table on a stage below. At the side of the auditorium, some guests were helping themselves to wine and hors d'oeuvres that had been laid out on tables. I felt conspicuous. If the cameraman sensed that I was no journalist, then the security people would also know. I headed to the men's washroom, entered a stall and copied a pose I had seen in a movie where a fugitive put his legs high up on the closed door so that a quick inspection by security staff would reveal an empty stall. Then I waited. Some men came in and used the washroom. It seemed my hiding place was working.

About ten minutes before the press conference was scheduled to begin, I went back to the auditorium, headed directly toward a smiling waiter, took a wineglass from his tray, then walked briskly to the closest cluster of guests. I knew none of them. They were discussing some political scandal, and I wasted no time offering an outrageous opinion. I was immediately swept into an animated conversation. A security guard nearby eyed me suspiciously, but I was laughing and talking with the other guests as if we were old friends, enjoying the mayor's wine.

Soon a signal was given for journalists to take their seats. I took a seat near the middle of a row. If I was going to ask a question, I would need to do it early in the press conference, and I felt my nervousness rising because I knew I had to come up with a good short question. I scribbled one quickly onto a piece of paper. I was ready.

Mayor Drapeau sat at a desk in the centre of the stage. After briefly welcoming reporters and guests, he was ready to entertain questions. I pressed a button on the desk and was acknowledged by the mayor, who asked for my name and for the name of my news organization. I gave my name and quickly slurred over the name of a local anti-poverty group's newsletter, then I quickly asked my question: "Why are you ignoring the plight of the poor in Montreal?" Mayor Drapeau got angry and demanded to know the name of my news organization. I asked him a second question: "Why are you giving priority to these Games while doing nothing about helping people in Montreal who are living in dire poverty?" By now, I could see several security guards rushing toward me. But I could relax; I had delivered our message. I was escorted out of the building by two tall, burly security men, each gripping one of my arms and briskly leading me out onto the sidewalk.

The next day, my impromptu questions were given headline coverage in Montreal's English-speaking newspaper. When I met up with my co-activists, they cheered me for upstaging the mayor. But despite receiving good publicity, nothing changed. The Games went ahead, the mayor leading the fanfare. The city provided no additional funds to help low-income Montrealers. Deep down, my frustration and sense of failure remained.

In fairness, our anti-poverty initiatives did win some limited victories. One such victory occurred after we demonstrated in front of a youth centre, protesting the inhumane conditions of these centres, which operated like harsh adult prisons. At that time, the War Measures Act had been invoked. All demonstrations in Montreal were banned, and the military had sent tanks and armed soldiers to Montreal to suppress threats of violence from Quebec nationalist militants. Fortunately, on the morning of our demonstration, it was raining, and many of us wore raincoats that allowed us to hide our signs and posters. The police were visible on Montreal's streets, their patrol cars slowly cruising through the city. We had invited the media to meet us at the entrance to the group home, and our group converged on its front steps just as the reporters arrived. We rang the bell and removed our placards from under our coats. When a surprised administrator answered the door, we asked to speak to the director of the home and gave her a press release that listed our demands for more humane conditions inside the home. The media gave us good coverage, and the Quebec Ministry of Health and Social Services provided a new budget for training youth counsellors who worked in these homes.

We experienced another small victory when an African-Canadian woman who was a member of our anti-poverty groups came to us with evidence that a landlord had refused to rent her an apartment because her skin was black. We leaped into action, and a group of us entered the council chamber in the Montreal municipality where that apartment building was located. We refused to leave when the municipal staff asked us to, and about twenty fully armed police officers entered the council chamber and positioned themselves just inside its curved wall, facing us as we faced them. The mayor sent his representative to tell us that a complaint about racism was within the jurisdiction of a Quebec provincial ministry; we should leave and go there. We replied that since the racism was taking place within his municipality, the mayor had an obligation to deal with the matter, and the media would be coming soon to ask him for his statement. Did he really want the media to report that he would do nothing to resolve the situation? When he asked what we wanted, we told him to intervene and find a solution that was acceptable to our African-Canadian member. An hour later, someone from the mayor's office came to the council chambers to tell us that the situation had been resolved to the new tenant's satisfaction, and the woman who had lodged the complaint soon arrived to let us know that she had been accepted as a tenant by the landlord.

We realized that anti-Black racism ran deep in Canada. Though it felt good to resolve one tenant's issue, it was a drop in the ocean. Perhaps my impatience was connected to my experience in Cleveland where we had made a dramatic difference by electing a Black American as mayor. It may also have been the contrast between a strong civil rights movement in the United States and what I saw as its fledgling counterpart in Canada. Perhaps my impatience was a result of the anti-climax sometimes experienced by social activists. While feeling some satisfaction that we had exposed an example of racism, we were interacting with an unsmiling mayor and a resentful landlord. At times, such negative responses made us vulnerable to backlash from people who were opposed to our activism and who ridiculed our efforts, calling us naive, immature and unrealistic troublemakers.

What helped to keep my spirits up were the small victories that we were achieving, plus the sense that we were taking action. In addition, there were strong ties of friendship among our activist groups.

After our monthly anti-poverty meetings, I would meet with my friend Jim Chang, and we would head downtown to Chinatown for savoury meals. This became a favourite routine, and the restaurants' waiters got to know us. Over jasmine tea, Jim and I shared our dreams. I told Jim that I was hoping to become a social work teacher at a university someday. He was very supportive. Jim told me he was going to get married, and I was thrilled for him. I knew Kathy, the woman he planned to marry, and she and Jim were a wonderful couple, both strong humanitarians and devoted members of their Baptist Church. He asked if I would be his best man for his wedding ceremony: I agreed and, to my surprise, I gave the funniest speech I ever delivered.

∼

While I was becoming more engaged in anti-poverty work in Montreal, I met my future life partner, Rhona Phillips, who opened up a whole new world for me. After I started working at the Montreal Council of Social Agencies, I realized that I wanted some connection to the Jewish community. When I had been a social work student at McGill, one of my student placements had been at the Jewish YMCA, the YMHA (Young Men's Hebrew Association), up on Westbury Avenue in the northern part of the city. I still had fond memories of the YMHA, so I visited the agency and noticed a sign on its bulletin board announcing that volunteers were needed to lead a group of youth with disabilities. I inquired and was interviewed by an administrator who then appointed me as one of the group's facilitators. After volunteering for several months, the administrator and his colleague arranged for me to meet Rhona on a blind date. Rhona, a native Montrealer, was a teacher in a school for children with severe cognitive impairments. When I met Rhona, I felt there was something special about her. I soon fell head over heels in love with her, and a new chapter of my life began.

Joys and Challenges

Rhona and I were having dinner at one of Montreal's romantic Spanish restaurants. Lights were dimmed, lit candles were on the tables, and soft music played as a backdrop our conversation, which was accompanied by a smooth bottle of wine. I had ordered a Spanish pizza, and Rhona was enjoying a different dish. I asked Rhona if she wanted to sample my pizza. She said, "Share it?" When I said yes, she asked if I wanted to share more than my pizza. We both knew she was asking about sharing our lives. I wanted to think about it more, but she gave me such an inviting smile, I could only say, "Of course." We decided we would get married in six months. We were both giddy, and not from the wine.

During the previous week, we had rented bicycles and rode to the harbour and other tourist haunts in Old Montreal. The more time we spent together, the more the chemistry between us was inviting us to deeper levels of intimacy. Rhona was cute, and her eyes penetrated my soul. When we talked, I realized that we shared many beliefs and values, and I sensed she could become a wonderful soulmate.

Rhona encouraged me to talk about my childhood years, sharing memories that I would typically run from. Though it still felt awkward, she helped me feel more comfortable talking about Baudour and the murder of my parents by the Nazis. Rhona was familiar with the Holocaust and shared what she knew about the various responses of Jewish scholars and philosophers toward that genocide. Having been raised in a traditional Jewish Orthodox home, she was more observant of Jewish practices, such as keeping kosher, than I was. Rhona's many cousins, aunties and other members of her large extended family were welcoming to me.

After our dinner at the Spanish restaurant, we wanted to tell her parents about our decision. We knew that they were spending the weekend near Sainte-Agathe, a small town north of Montreal. They had in recent summers rented what they called "the shack" — a small, wooden structure whose paint had peeled off over a decade ago; it had two tiny bedrooms with mattresses that sank to the floor and furniture that had seen better days. The area was surrounded by trees and bushes, creating a quiet retreat from city living. Various family members, visiting for the day, would put up their lawn chairs on the grass and read or doze off.

As we arrived at the shack, Rhona's father was heading inside carrying an armful of logs. Rhona greeted him and announced that we were planning to be married in November. He stopped walking, his arms went limp, and all the logs he was carrying fell onto the rickety porch with a loud crash. I worried that this was a sign of his disapproval, but I quickly realized I was wrong, as he rushed inside to tell Rhona's mother, Aida. They both came back outside with wide smiles and insisted on giving us each a huge hug. Rhona's mum asked Rhona what kind of a wedding she was considering, and without hesitating, Rhona answered, "Obnoxious." Her mum squealed with delight. Rhona meant that her mother could organize our wedding the way she wanted. "The important thing is we are getting married," she said to me. I agreed.

A few months before our wedding, Rhona asked me which household chores I was going to do as we established our home. In previous conversations we had both agreed that within our marriage we would carry out egalitarian decision-making processes, but now her question made me squirm. As a teenager in Ottawa, my experience of family life was of men reading the newspaper and otherwise relaxing as women cleaned, cooked, served meals and washed dishes. At the time, it seemed perfectly normal. Rhona asked me again: What would I sign up for? Cooking? Laundry? Buying the food? Cleaning house? After some uneasy conversations, we settled on my doing the dishes, buying food and doing some of the cleaning.

At times, we receive nourishing surprises from glimpses into nature's gifts when we least expect it. On November 27, 1971, Rhona and I were married in a Montreal synagogue. As the time came for us to leave our wedding celebration, we hugged our guests and bundled up in warm winter coats. As we stepped into the cold night air, large fluffy snowflakes, like huge white feathers, were slowly descending all around us in a gentle wind. We walked toward my small car across fresh snow that felt like a soft blanket underfoot. Reflecting the light from street lamps, the countless tiny crystals on the ground were shining and sparkling like jewels, as if winking at us. Lifted up off the ground by gusts of wind, these gentle, white, crystal lights danced all around us, invigorating the intimacy of love that Rhona and I were feeling.

Married life brought joy. As a couple, we grew close to Rhona's family. I did my share of housework, and Rhona was glad I was able to change the gender pattern that I had learned from my family and from Western society's normative values at the time. Rhona wanted to see changes within her family as well. As Passover approached, she talked about how the seder was entirely run by the males in her family. Her father or uncle would read from the Haggadah, which tells the biblical story of the exodus of Jews from slavery in Egypt. The reading of the Haggadah is interspersed with rituals such as eating matzah, drinking wine and sampling bitter herbs to recall the bitterness of slavery. Rhona felt we should have more participation from everyone at her parents' seder.

The Passover meal was to be held at Rhona's parents' place in the neighbourhood of Côte Saint-Luc. As guests started to arrive,

I approached Rhona's father, Sydney, and asked him if everyone at the seder could take a turn to read from the Haggadah. His reply was quick and firm: No. He had led the Passover ritual for years, and he would continue to do so, without anyone's help. Rhona was disappointed.

Rhona's parents had kindly agreed to invite my friend Jim Chang and his new wife, Kathy, to this seder. As Jim and Kathy and Rhona's family all gathered in the dining room, dressed for the special occasion, the atmosphere was jovial and festive. A delicious aroma of simmering chicken soup wafted out from the kitchen next to the dining room.

Sydney gave a signal for us to find our seats and began conducting the seder. We reached the Four Questions, which were intended to encourage children to ask questions about the seder and the story of redemption, and Rhona's brother chanted them: Why is this meal different from other meals? Why matzah? After he had finished, I stood up and said, "I would like to ask a fifth question. If this is the holiday of freedom, why don't we practise it here, tonight, at this seder?" I turned to face Rhona's three aunts and asked, "Would you like to take a turn at reading from the Haggadah instead of just having one person read from it?" They replied, "What a wonderful idea!" Rhona's uncle responded by saying that freedom doesn't mean just doing anything we want. I agreed, but surely it wasn't wrong for everyone to take a turn at reading the story of the Exodus from the Haggadah?

I glanced at Sydney, who looked at me with a sour expression, then I suggested that we go around the table, each person taking a turn to read. I looked at Rhona. She was mortified. She later told me that she had asked herself: *If my father throws Ben out of the house, do I go with him or stay?* Then Rhona's teenage brother, Jimmy, blurted out, "Why are we reading all this crap?" Sydney glared at Jimmy and told him to respect his father. I cringed and felt the embarrassment of Jim and Kathy.

We got through the rest of the seder, all of us tiptoeing, on our best behaviour. When it was time to serve the food, Rhona's mother told us that the chicken had burnt because of everyone taking a turn to read. Sydney sent me another sour face. As the food was served, our hunger subsided, and Sydney calmed down. After the meal and a few songs, Rhona and I politely excused ourselves and scampered out before anything else could go wrong.

A year later, on Passover, Rhona and I were living in Calgary. We phoned Rhona's parents to ask how their seder went, and Aida was excited to tell Rhona, "Daddy made a wonderful suggestion that everyone could take a turn reading from the Haggadah, in English or in Hebrew." Everyone had been enthusiastic about his novel decision.

When Rhona got off the phone and told me what her mother had said, we both enjoyed hearty laughter. I took this to mean that I was forgiven by Sydney for last year's turbulent seder.

Rhona and I moved to Calgary in 1973, after I was offered a position to teach social work at the University of Calgary. We were ecstatic for several reasons. Even back in Cleveland, I had dreamed of teaching social work at a university. We had also seen pictures of the Rockies, and now we were able to experience the splendour of those majestic mountains with their snow-covered peaks. We never tired of walking along well-marked trails, pausing to gaze at emerald lakes and marvel at white mountain goats bouncing up hillsides between rocks and trees.

Though I had been given a warm welcome by Rhona's large extended family, Rhona felt that being away from Montreal would allow us to develop our own way of being a couple and a family. Our two daughters were born in Calgary, and we lived there long enough for them to start school. Rhona and I knew we eventually would return to Central Canada to be closer to Rhona's family in Montreal and to my adoptive family, as well as to Frantz and Minn, who had moved to Ottawa. Meanwhile, we enjoyed frequent visits from Rhona's parents, who were happy to babysit and spoil our kids during the ten years we were in Calgary.

My Inner Life Grows

To support the development of my inner life, I had been reading and re-reading books by Abraham Joshua Heschel, a wise and spiritual Orthodox rabbi whose writings made God accessible to me. Yes, God was invisible, mysterious, beyond human comprehension, but as Heschel described it, God's love was also present to us if we allowed it to enter our lives. As I reflected on this teaching, I made a conscious effort to welcome in God's love.

After Rhona and I had our first child, whom we named Mira Elsa — Elsa after my birth mother — I became far more conscious of my inner life. For many years, I had been aware of my inner thoughts and feelings, but like most people, I found my inner life only came to the forefront of my consciousness at specific times. As a new father, I imagined that my parents, wherever their spirits hovered, were pleased to know that Rhona had given birth. I was sad they could not be physically with me, yet I felt their souls were very much present. I also experienced a deep spiritual presence, as if God too was smiling upon us. We also felt the support of my Ottawa family. Rhona and I had taken a course that explained the intricate development of the fetus inside the mother's body. As I held Mira soon after she was born and after we brought her home, I could only marvel in awe at the mystery of this beautiful new life.

Jewish tradition has a welcome ceremony for baby boys but not for baby girls, so, with the help of friends, Rhona and I created a welcome ceremony for Mira Elsa. We held the ceremony in our Calgary apartment and invited friends and family. Rhona's family flew in from Montreal. As our guests arrived, we gave each of them a script we had written for the ceremony. We distributed small candles for guests to hold and turned off the overhead light; the room became magical in the twilight, and guests sighed in unison at the sudden beauty of the soft glow.

Our ceremony included a thanksgiving to God for all of us being able to be present. Rhona and I said a blessing and sang a song in Hebrew, welcoming Mira Elsa and explaining her name. We invited Rhona's parents to read short excerpts from the Torah, and each guest was invited to read a blessing. Then we shared a *l'chaim* over wine and had some refreshments. After our welcoming ceremony, I felt a deep sense of gratitude for the many blessings in our lives. Mira grew and thrived.

One harsh Calgary winter, when Mira was two or three years old, I slipped on some ice as I loaded her into her car seat. Mira fell to the ground and began to scream. I couldn't tell if she was seriously injured, so I quickly secured her in the car seat and drove to the emergency department at a nearby hospital, Mira crying all the way. My heart was pounding as I pulled up to the emergency entrance. Inside, there were many people sitting on benches waiting to be seen by doctors. Numerous medical staff were in motion, busy doing their work. Yet in the middle of this crowd of humanity swirling around me, I felt utterly alone. I was ashamed of not having been more careful. I thought back to the moment I had slipped on ice and dropped Mira. I was worried sick that she might have a life-threatening injury. Or had I caused a permanent disability? I tried to imagine how I could have moved differently so as not to drop her. But no matter how much I revisited the moment, I could not change what had happened.

In the midst of this anguish, I suddenly felt a presence. Was it Rhona? She had been at work. Did she find out I was here and come? No, this was a spiritual presence. There was no voice, but I heard reassuring messages. It was as if God was talking to me: "No matter what the doctors find, you are not alone. There is no need to blame yourself. You did not intend any harm. Remember, you are not alone."

I was on the edge of tears, but for the sake of Mira, I pulled myself together. A nurse came across the room, lifted Mira gently and turned her body to face me. Then Mira's eyes looked into mine as if to say, "I'm okay," and she blew me a kiss. Here was my young daughter, knowing exactly what I needed in that moment, lifting me from the depths of my shame and panic. Her love helped me regain my balance, and I felt stronger. The doctors told me that Mira was fine, and in the days that followed, our doctor concluded there was no concussion. I thanked God that Mira was okay.

Four years after Mira was born, we were expecting our second child. Medical tests told us that our baby was to be a girl. Rhona and I picked out a name: Naomi Tamara. Naomi because we liked the softness of the name and Tamara after my father's Hebrew name, Mathias. About one week before Naomi's birth, we received the results of routine tests that indicated that Naomi was going to be born with a severe abnormality. We were both in a daze.

My inner life became activated, on full alert. I felt God was present, letting me know I was not alone and giving me the courage to reassure Rhona that she was not alone. Yes, Rhona was with me, and I could feel her love, how she was physically close. But God's love was different, close yet distant at the same time: it was a strong, sacred presence all around me, lifting me up so I felt balanced and able to say what I wanted to say. I felt God's love pushing away my insecurities and fears and shoring up my confidence.

Rhona and I had a friend who was a pediatrician, and he offered to check out the lab results. He soon reported that there had been an error; there were no indications of any abnormalities. Our friend promised he would be nearby at Rhona's second childbirth, and soon after Naomi was born, he gave us the exhilarating news: she was fine. Rhona and I were ecstatic to bring a healthy Naomi home, and we had a similar welcome ceremony for her as we had for Mira.

Naomi grew. As with Mira, Rhona and I shared the night feeding, Rhona breastfed her, and I fed her with a bottle. Mira enjoyed being the big sister, while Naomi imitated the way Mira moved, talked and played.

One day, Mira, Naomi and I were playing on the living room floor, when something funny happened, and all three of us burst out laughing. As Naomi's mouth opened wide with laughter, I could see the full range of her new teeth. They were tiny, white and gorgeous. But then I got a shock. My imagination was triggered, and at first, I wasn't sure what I was seeing, but as I focused my vision, I was repelled. I saw the outline of several corpses and skeletons with white bones strewn on the ground. Then I saw a close-up of two corpses, partly covered with soil, each with a row of white-grey teeth. I sensed that these were the teeth of my parents.

I left the room, feeling the tears coming but holding them in until I was out of sight of my daughters. In the bathroom, I washed my face. I was bewildered. Furious questions arose, demanding answers: Why had that image come to me now? What did it mean? Aside from undermining my joy, was my inner life seeking to release my anger? I did want to scream at the Nazi murderers: "You right-wing bastards! You tried to wipe us out. But you scumbags failed! We Jews are still here. We have survived. We are growing. And look — we are thriving!"

I wondered why my inner life was trying to remind me of what I desperately wanted to ignore. I knew that now was not the time for me to figure out why this image came to me. I realized that I had been affected by the murder of my parents and the genocide of so many others, but I had courses to teach, reading lists to prepare, and I wanted to do my share of household chores and also be supportive to Rhona and our daughters. I had to accept that some things would need to remain unresolved for the time being.

Indigenous Resistance

In Calgary, I was pulled into a conflict that was both familiar and totally new to me.

On November 28, 1974, about thirty Indigenous men, women and children began their occupation of the Calgary Indian Affairs office. While I had participated in social actions to draw public attention to injustices, I was not familiar with protests by Indigenous Peoples who had experienced the specific injustices linked to their identity.

I had met the Indigenous leaders of this protest in their office in a run-down community centre in downtown Calgary soon after my arrival in the city. Roy Little Chief, Urban Calling Last and Nelson Small Legs, Jr. had welcomed me because I was accompanied by someone they knew and respected, Professor Nelson Gutnick from the University of Calgary. Professor Gutnick had earned immense respect among Indigenous leaders when he was employed by the Department of Indian Affairs and was known as a trustworthy friend of "Indians," what Indigenous Peoples were commonly called at that time.

At that meeting, I learned that the Calgary Urban Treaty Indian Alliance had received a short-term grant from the Department of Indian Affairs to hire eleven Indigenous counsellors to assist First Nations people who were moving to Calgary from nearby reserves. Nelson Small Legs, Jr. asked Professor Gutnick how the University of Calgary could support their work. In response, Professor Gutnick convened a number of supporters from the university and elsewhere. Joan Ryan[1] from the university's Department of Anthropology suggested that our group of supporters document details about the mistreatment of clients by Indian Affairs, which we began to do.

Before the occupation of the offices of Indian Affairs, Gutnick invited a newspaper reporter to hear directly about the experiences of the Calgary Urban Treaty Indian Alliance in trying to stop Indian Affairs' mistreatment of their clients. Gutnick would also be the contact person who would stay in touch with the demonstrators during the protest. Our support group agreed that we should seek help from the Indigenous Chiefs of Treaty 7, consisting of five First Nations in Southern Alberta: the Siksika (Blackfoot), Kainai (Blood), Piikani (Peigan), Stoney-Nakoda, and Tsuut'ina (Sarcee). I was asked to keep Treaty 7 Chiefs up to date on developments and was dispatched to meet with the leadership at one of their Band Council meetings just as the occupation began.

As protesters occupied the Indian Affairs office, the staff wasted no time in locking up their file cabinets, taking their personal belongings and quickly leaving, while the office managers contacted the police. Calgary's mayor was notified and issued a media bulletin calling the demonstrators "terrorists" and demanding that the police charge in and forcibly remove the demonstrators.

I became frightened. I had heard about the police in the United States charging into a meeting of Black Power militants and killing them. Might such police brutality be repeated in Calgary? Aggravating my fear was not knowing if the police were planning to punish me for being part of the informal support group that was connected to the Calgary Urban Treaty Indian Alliance. I grew even more tense

---

1   Joan Ryan would go on to write *Wall of Words: The Betrayal of the Urban Indian* (Toronto: Peter Martin, 1978).

when I heard a rumour that the demonstrators had snuck a rifle into the Indian Affairs office. I was frantic, insisting that Professor Gutnick meet with Roy Little Chief at a location outside the occupied office to caution him about the severe risks. If the police concluded that the demonstrators had weapons, they would have the perfect excuse to charge in with guns blazing and cause a massacre. Roy told Gutnick that it was good to keep the other side on edge. Roy later told me that no rifle had been smuggled into the Indian Affairs office. He was smiling as he told me this, as if to say he wanted to keep others on edge. I told him that the edge had put all the demonstrators at risk.

Just when I feared that the worst-case scenario would happen, the police chief made a stunning public statement that, in his professional opinion, the situation required patience, caution and negotiation rather than the use of force. He was praised by the media for his wisdom. I could barely believe that the police chief was openly disobeying Calgary's mayor. My comfortable stereotype about "redneck" Albertans was shattered. True, the mayor still fit my stereotype of anti-Indigenous racism, but at the crucial moment, it was not true that the mayor could compel the police to carry out a violent, racist attack on Indigenous protesters. The group I was in that was supporting the protesters not only cheered, we went into high gear and hit the phones. We reached out to as many people as possible, asking them to phone the Calgary police and thank the police chief for choosing negotiations instead of violence. Within two days of the police chief's statement, about seventy phone calls were made from our support group to Calgary's police office.

Meanwhile, we received more good news. Treaty 7 Chiefs had decided to meet with the demonstrators and publicly support their occupation. Within forty-eight hours after it started, the occupation ended. The *Calgary Herald* provided the public with extensive stories investigating the bureaucratic runaround inflicted on clients by the Department of Indian Affairs.

Nelson Small Legs, Jr. thanked me and others for our timely support. He was a tall figure, with two neat braids of dark hair flowing down on each side of his face, resting in front of his shoulders. Though others from our support group knew him much better than I did, I was growing to enjoy his easy sense of humour and friendly smile. His tone of voice was soft, yet I sensed a tough determination that came from deep inside his being.

Despite a successful demonstration, which ended well, the grievances against the Department of Indian Affairs were not resolved, and local Indigenous activists continued to criticize the Department of Indian Affairs. One day, Nelson Small Legs, Jr. loaded his rifle, dressed himself in full Indigenous regalia and shot himself in the heart. He left a note saying that he was giving up his life in protest and demanding a public investigation of Indian Affairs to stop the harm to his community.

At his funeral, aside from a large crowd of Indigenous mourners, a spirited white horse, almost wild, accompanied Nelson Small Legs, Jr.'s body to his grave. It was as if his spirit was now in the horse, wild with hope that all of us would hear his message. We had lost a gentle soul, someone with a message we needed to hear.

Human Nature and Suffering

My deepening journey into my inner life offered a way for me to address the shocking death of Nelson Small Legs, Jr. I began to realize that it took tremendous courage for him to take his life in an attempt to open the eyes of the people who were contributing to the suffering of his community. I was beginning to see how suffering was not inevitable, though I was still hearing excuses for racism: "It's just human nature." It was a mantra I had encountered in the United States as a justification not only for the Vietnam War, but for all wars — "just human nature." It was also a justification I had heard in Montreal: poverty was explained as inevitable — "It's just the nature of things."

Breaking this link between human nature and suffering became possible for me as I plunged into Jewish learning. Rhona and I agreed to run a conversion course for people interested in becoming Jewish. The course was sponsored by Calgary's Jewish Reform movement. Rhona was invited to teach because of her extensive knowledge of biblical texts, Jewish history and Jewish philosophers through the ages. Rhona wanted me to lead group discussions because of my familiarity with teaching mature university students. She also decided to have sessions at our home so that she could involve students in experiences such as baking challah for Shabbat, conducting a Havdalah ceremony with its spices and fire to welcome the week, and sitting inside the sukkah that we had built in our backyard to experience the fragile nature of our lives from a Jewish angle.

Rhona and I met regularly to plan the program, which included my learning more about Jewish history and philosophy. It was a steep learning curve for me. As I entered into these studies, I was especially interested in finding Jewish teachings that addressed human suffering.

As I learned more about biblical stories and their lessons, I started to realize that Jewish biblical narratives had emerged in a world of brutal living conditions, when human suffering was commonplace and the world was filled with violence, racism and slavery. It was a time when patriarchs and kings ruled with the iron fist of absolute authority and when frequent famines were death sentences for many people. I could well imagine that life in such a world meant being totally absorbed in locating the material requirements for survival. My ancestors had faced hostile conditions, but during this period of early recorded history, there also emerged a human consciousness of God as a non-material, spiritual dimension. The Jewish Bible, the Torah, provided a description of how the Jewish people reacted to this emerging spiritual awareness. I began to recognize that it was nothing short of a miracle that in such an era, when suffering was rampant, when the need for survival would be all-absorbing, there emerged a spiritual awakening that opposed the immense suffering associated with the prevailing practice of ruthless coercion and tyrannical control.

Studying biblical texts, listening to rabbis and reading books by Jewish philosophers, I developed new perspectives on human nature and suffering. I recognized that the biblical Moses and other ancient Jewish prophets were inspired to question conditions of slavery and cruelty, which would have been considered inevitable in the times they lived. Leaders of other religions also challenged human behaviours such as greed, violence and aggression. These leaders were joined by artists, poets, musicians and writers and others with compassionate souls who understood that it was foolish to extol violence and aggression because such behaviour destroyed not only humans, but also the humanity of the perpetrators. If greed, violence and aggression were perceived to be caused by human nature, the suffering they caused would also be seen as inevitable. But these spiritual innovators were saying that we humans could do better. We were not predestined to inflict harm upon others. Religious faith based in love and caring could move us away from harming others. However, perpetrators of violence, aggression and other forms of suffering do not look kindly to their power being challenged.

As I journeyed deeper within my inner life, I recognized that throughout history, right up to contemporary times, there have been many initiatives by people opposing suffering. Today, there are the Black Lives Matter and #MeToo movements; Indigenous land defenders at Standing Rock, North Dakota and throughout Turtle Island; human rights activists who advocate for people struggling against poverty, and for disability rights and gender equality. These advocates want justice for people with different sexualities and sexual expressions. They have condemned anti-Black racism, Islamophobia, antisemitism and anti-Asian racism. They have railed against anti-unionism and tax evasion by the super-rich. These countless advocates are often anonymous, unsung heroes in the trenches of day-to-day struggles to bring about more social justice. I started to recognize that Nelson Small Legs, Jr. was one such hero among those striving for justice within their communities and beyond.

My inner life was becoming impatient, urging me to alert my fellow activists that we needed a wider strategy to undermine suffering. If we continued to believe that human nature was predisposed to aggression, violence and greed, then suffering would be forever sealed into our future. But if we could change such perceptions, if we could see that human nature could encourage cooperation, kindness and respect for the diversity of life, large swaths of suffering could be stopped.

As Jews in the Holocaust were confronted with violence and mass murder, some drew upon their religious beliefs and prayed to God to intervene. They prayed for mighty miracles to block Nazis from carrying out genocide. When those miracles did not happen, and instead the Nazis continued carrying out their diabolical schemes, some Jews felt betrayed by God. Others, like me when I was a young adult, concluded that to believe in God was to believe in a simplistic fairy tale.

As I studied more Jewish history and philosophy, I began to feel that these responses were premised on a specific version of God — a God who had the capacity to produce miracles here and now to instantly save innocent people from massive harm and destruction. This version of God's power had become a foundation of Jewish faith, and it persists to this day. Yet Rabbi Abraham Joshua Heschel presented a different view of God. As I studied his writings, I began to let go of blaming God for failing to stop the Holocaust.

Rabbi Heschel narrowly escaped the Holocaust and immigrated to the United States in 1940. I admired him because he was a social activist and protested against America's involvement in the Vietnam War. He marched with Martin Luther King, Jr. in demonstrations that challenged the anti-Black racism that permeated North America. I understood from Heschel's writings that he believed that it was not God but human beings who had failed to prevent the Nazi murder of Jews and many others. Heschel believed that people had failed to respond with compassion and moral leadership to a scourge of severe injustices, which had inflicted immense suffering on large sections of the population.

Heschel was no newcomer to suffering. Aside from suffering in his personal life from the murder of his family members by the Nazis, he had focused on suffering in his academic writing. I was taken by his writings about the Jewish prophets of antiquity who had harshly criticized my ancestors for worshipping fastidiously in their Jerusalem Temple while trampling on the poor, ignoring the plight of widows and orphans, and cheating in business. Heschel noted how one of the ancient Jewish prophets, Jeremiah, viewed my ancestors:

> They have become fat and sleek;
> They pass beyond the bounds of wickedness,
> And they prosper.
> They will not judge the case of the orphan,
> Nor give a hearing to the plea of the needy.[1]

From Heschel I learned about how the ancient prophets wanted to stop suffering and how central to Jewish thinking was the idea that humans had choices. To stop suffering, humans had to step up; it was not only up to God.

Thanks to Rabbi Heschel, my inner life no longer accused God of failing to stop the Nazis' crimes against humanity. I began to understand that God expected humans to initiate and make ethical choices to stop suffering. Through my readings, I was being drawn to a spirituality that built on traditional Jewish practice while moving toward a far more inclusive version of Judaism. This meant making gender equality and an acceptance of different forms of sexuality and gender expressions a central part of my Jewish religious beliefs. It also meant actively supporting progressive politics aimed at stopping all types of suffering at their root. While the Holocaust mainly targeted Jews, Nazi violence had also targeted homosexuals, people of colour, dissenters against fascism, people with disabilities and other people who were "different." The Nazis spread their horrific cruelty so widely that I felt empathy toward a variety of people who were also dehumanized and abused through violent Nazi aggression.

---

1 Reproduced from the *Tanakh: The Holy Scriptures* by permission of the University of Nebraska Press. Copyright 1985 by The Jewish Publication Society, Philadelphia.

As a deeper political awareness became part of my identity as an adult, my inner life came to accept that spirituality and progressive politics could work well together. They both could accelerate a change of attitudes, away from a vision of human nature as inevitably drawn to greed, racism, violence and war, and toward a new understanding of human nature that called for the prevention of violence against anyone, anywhere.

Frantz and Minn

In the early 1980s, I took a sabbatical from the University of Calgary and moved to Toronto with Rhona and our two daughters for six months. Frantz and Minn were still living in Ottawa, and we were invited to visit them there. When we arrived at their home for dinner one evening, Rhona joined Minn in the kitchen where they began talking about recipes. Frantz invited me and our daughters to see the flowers he was growing in his greenhouse. We climbed to the second floor and admired bunches of flowers of different shapes and sizes growing in a warm room beneath a glass ceiling. Frantz then led us into an office, where he opened up an encyclopedia and showed us some of the flowers he was growing. He flipped through the encyclopedia and showed us a picture of African Indigenous people wearing traditional headdress.

I wondered if they were happy and said so. Frantz became defensive, saying that the Belgian government felt a special responsibility to protect the hunting grounds of these tribes. I asked Frantz if the Belgian Congo had participated in the slave trade, and he responded that some cultural practices, such as Jews not eating pork, were silly because they were based on superstition rather than rationality. Now I became annoyed. I guessed he had wanted to eat pork for dinner and Minn had refused.

When Minn called us to come for dinner, I went by myself. I thought that Mira and Naomi would prefer to continue exploring the exotic artifacts on the office shelves, such as artistic wood carvings from Africa and a wide African drum hanging on the wall. It took Frantz a while to cajole our daughters to come downstairs, and when they came to the table, he seemed annoyed that he had to do it. I told myself: That's what's missing in our relationship. He really does not know our kids.

Before we arrived at Frantz and Minn's home, Rhona and I had talked about how our relationship with them lacked a certain authenticity, and I was going to see if we could somehow improve that. So when we had all gathered at the table, I expressed disappointment that they had not visited us in Toronto.

Frantz said they had been busy organizing their garden. I said that he was retired and could have made time to visit us with Minn. Frantz became visibly upset. His face turned red in a furious rage, and he said that my comments were inappropriate. I said that my comments were trying to improve our relationship. When he abruptly left the table, I realized that the meal was over and that we were meant to leave. As Rhona and the children and I went to the front door, Frantz shouted, "Don't ever talk to me again!"

At first, I experienced disbelief. But as time went on and Frantz continued to refuse speaking with me, I was devastated. Rhona and I, as well as Mira, reached out to him, hoping that he would re-open communication with me. Though he eventually communicated with Mira, he kept the door firmly shut against Rhona and me. After months and months of our reaching out through letters and phone calls, he remained adamant — no more contact!

I remembered that years earlier, Frantz had had a disagreement with his sister, and he had also broken off all communication with her. It was my adoptive brother Sid who reminded me that Frantz had been a political prisoner. He had been a leader of an anti-Nazi partisan group that blew up bridges, interrupted Nazi supply lines and provided intelligence to the British during the Nazi occupation of Belgium; the group was known as the Secret Army. The Gestapo were known for their use of torture, and my brother suggested that such an experience could easily lead to emotional imbalance.

In any case, I was deeply hurt by Frantz shutting down communications between us. I wished I could have said things differently at that dinner. I had hoped to improve our relationship, but with hindsight, I realized I had been clumsy in what I did. After living in Canada for decades, Frantz and Minn move back to Belgium and settled in a rural suburb of Brussels.

Facing the Holocaust

When we moved back to Toronto from Calgary in 1983, I was happy to be closer to our extended families. We could drive to Montreal to visit Rhona's family and to Ottawa to visit my family. Our children could spend some time with their Ottawa grandmother (Granny) and also enjoy their grandparents (Bubby and Zaida) in Montreal. We did those trips several times a year. Though Frantz and Minn had moved back to Belgium, we still enjoyed going to Ottawa because of visits to my mother and my two brothers who, with their gracious wives, very much welcomed us into their homes.

In 1992, my adoptive mother, Greta Cohen, having lived a full life, passed away in Ottawa at the age of ninety-one. I was saddened, but I was also comforted by the fact that in her old age she had not suffered from any prolonged, painful illness. I also knew that she had felt well loved by me and by many family members and friends.

After the death of an immediate family member, there is a custom among traditional Jews to go to synagogue services to recite a special prayer, Kaddish, daily for eleven months. I decided to honour my adoptive mother in this way. Soon, I settled into the routine of attending morning services at a chapel on the lower floor of a large synagogue about one block from where we lived. There were usually fifteen to twenty other congregants also attending. We would find our places in the rows of long wooden pews, and the prayer leader would chant the first line of each prayer. I would stand up, sit down and chant the prayers along with everyone else.

I was becoming used to saying the Kaddish prayer: it is a short prayer, taking just a couple of minutes in the services when mourners stand up and recite it in unison, out loud, in Aramaic. While I would recite the Kaddish, I would also meditate on memories of my adoptive mother. I appreciated this quiet space in advance of the daily rush of demands and activities. Here, I could grieve for Greta. After about a month, I decided to sharpen the focus of my meditation on the many ways she had shown her love for me. I could easily conjure up images of her smiling face and approving eyes. I reflected on her willingness to make room for me within her immediate family. As I grew into an adult, she was also able to accept my social justice advocacy. For weeks upon weeks, I thanked God for my being able to feel her love as I reflected on these memories.

As the months rolled by, my inner life told me that I was close to accepting her passing. With several months left to say Kaddish, I became acutely aware that I had never grieved for my original parents. I had consciously and unconsciously repressed, evaded and postponed grieving for them. My fear had blocked me. I did not want to think about their horrid deaths. But now something had changed. Perhaps encouraged by Greta's love and her acceptance of me, I now intentionally guided my reflections and meditation to slowly and cautiously drift to memories of my mother and father.

Being in a place of worship, it was natural for me to turn to God and say: *Please be with me as I embark on this new journey.* Carefully, I began asking myself what I remembered. I had many good memories from being with my parents for the first five years of my life. Could I remember the various facial expressions of my mother, of my father? I remembered my mother's sweet hugs. I had many more memories of her than of my father, though I knew he cared about me. What were some specific events I could recall? There was one time when they were both upset, shouting at each other. But their anger was not aimed at each other: it was as if there was a threat outside of our apartment, which at the time, I did not understand.

I also remembered them regularly bringing me to a park near where we lived in Brussels. One of them would push my stroller, and I would get out and play in a large sandbox. Sometimes I played with other children, but often I played by myself, the only child in that sandbox.

I remembered a few neatly wrapped gift packages on a high shelf that I had found when I stood up for the first time in my crib, surprising my parents. These gifts were intended for my birthday. I cried when my parents told me I had to wait until my birthday to open them. They hugged and consoled me, and I felt loved.

After being bolstered by good memories about my parents, I placed my large tallis over my head, and I asked God: *Please stay with me.* Then, for the first time, I tried in a purposeful way to imagine what my parents had encountered as prisoners inside those disgusting Nazi factories of murder. I found myself trying to shield them from the cruel dehumanization and continuous humiliation inflicted on them by the Nazi guards. I empathized with their daily experience of wallowing in filth, being overworked, underfed, and surrounded by cruel insults and terrible illnesses. As I entered that ocean of brutality, I witnessed the systematic Nazi efforts to destroy all sense of decency, humanity and hope. But I also witnessed a series of tiny, secret acts of rebellion, of human caring, such as holding up another prisoner during roll call to avoid them being sent to the gas chambers, or sharing food with a starving neighbour — I envisioned everyday quiet acts of resistance that offered the emotional nourishment that helped some prisoners survive, acts that could be seen as evidence of God's quiet presence in those dungeons of Nazi hate.

Yet I felt powerless. I wanted to join this resistance but realized I could offer no protection. The strange thought came to me: I was now much older than my parents had been when they were yanked away from me by the Nazis. I tried to imagine what their thoughts about me might have been, their hopes for my survival and for my future. What would my parents have wished for my life while they were confined in that Nazi hell? What might I do that would offer them relief? Since they had no voice, I could be their voice. Since I had not been imprisoned, I could try to do what they could not do while in captivity. Whatever defiance against mistreatment they had demonstrated within captivity, I could try to carry it further because I was not in captivity. If I could do that, I told myself, I would be amplifying their resistance against the violation of decency that they and so many others had to endure.

As I thought about such a goal for myself, I suddenly realized how familiar it was. In one way or another, I had been striving toward such a goal for many years. Going into social work was one of the building blocks toward that goal. So was my volunteering to support voter registration of Black voters in Cleveland. I had been reaching for the undoing of the violations caused by racism. By opposing the Vietnam War, I had been reaching for an end to the violations from unjustifiable military violence.

I found myself talking with my parents as I imagined them in those horrendous places. Not talking physically, with words, but it was as if my soul was joining with their souls across time. I was surprised that I could again feel their love from long ago in a way that was more than just a memory. I could feel the love as I sat in that Toronto chapel, as if they were expressing it right in front of me and all around me. It felt so real; it was like a strong structure built long ago yet still standing, higher than the tallest mountain, deeper than the past and wider than the present — offering me shelter. It was a healing, comforting love that I now felt around me and inside me.

As I drifted between my inner life and awareness of sitting near others on the long wooden pews in the synagogue's chapel, I was thankful that my prayer shawl was large enough to cover my entire head. I now shifted my focus away from the love of my parents for me and began imagining my parents being killed in Auschwitz, one of the notorious sites of mass murder. I imagined accompanying my mother first, then my father, during their final minutes before their lives were ripped away from them. I told myself not to gaze too long upon the images that came to me, like those I had seen in books, of corpses piled high or strewn about in open graves. It was one thing to look at photographs, an entirely different experience for me to wonder whether one of those corpses was my mother or father.

I imagined my mother being forced along with others into a gas chamber. I saw its heavy doors being firmly locked from the outside, followed by the poison gas raining down from numerous showerheads attached to the ceiling. I imagined the poison gas filling the tightly sealed chamber, extinguishing the oxygen that my mother needed to breathe, causing her to lose consciousness and fall to the ground until she could move no more. I needed to pause for a few seconds to see my mother's body lying still on the ground, to finally face her death, to feel what I had tried for so long to deny.

I then imagined my father being taken to a different gas chamber. In my imagining, he decided to rebel and ran in the opposite direction. I witnessed a hail of bullets fired from machine guns aimed at him by cold-blooded Nazi enforcers. I saw my father stumbling to the ground, surrounded by a widening pool of blood, then become motionless as his life was violently taken away from him. Here too, I needed to pause to see my father's body lying motionless on the ground, to finally face his death, to feel what I had tried for so long to deny.

Now that I had fully witnessed my mother and father being murdered, I was able to let my tears quietly flow. The floodgates of grief that I had carefully suppressed for so many decades were now, at last, bursting open. Many tears came, and I welcomed them, hidden from others beneath my tallis in that Toronto synagogue.

I felt more balanced as my fears dissipated. I had been afraid of facing my parents' pain. I had feared my reaction and the pain of empathizing with their experience as their lives were brutally yanked away from them. I could feel these fears were now vanishing in direct proportion to my ability to face their murders. I thanked God for staying with me as I went through this, while my resistance to facing their deaths was finally melting away. Looking back, I now better understand how, with God's presence, love can conquer fear and inspire the courage needed to enter fearsome places. I felt I had come home by honouring my Jewish identity. I was grieving for my losses in a Jewish way, saying Kaddish for my parents with other members from my community, while others were saying Kaddish to remember their loved ones.

Along with my grief, I also felt intense gratitude to my parents for arranging for my identity to be hidden from those who wanted to harm me and murder me. When I sensed the presence of my parents, I was conscious that there were no direct words from them; there was no voice. I could only feel their love — strong, clear and deep. As my tears subsided, I felt I could breathe more easily, like a long-standing burden was lifting from my shoulders and evaporating into the clouds above.

After I mourned the murders of my mother and father, I was able to honour other victims of the Nazi genocide — members of my extended family who had lived in Romania: my paternal great-grandmother, Rosa Lazarovitch; my uncle Joseph Carniol; and my aunt Malvine (Molly) Carniol. I also grieved for the six million, all the Jews who were murdered during the Holocaust by Nazis and their local Jew-hating collaborators.

Revisiting the Past

Though Frantz was no longer speaking with me, I maintained a connection with Minn throughout the years. Our daughter Mira and my brother Sid also stayed in touch with Frantz. Mira visited with Frantz and Minn several times over nine years, bringing back original documents, letters and photographs, and Mira and Naomi both visited Minn in Belgium after Frantz died. In 1997, when I heard from Sid and Mira that Frantz had passed away, I immediately sent a note to Minn, saying that I was sorry for her loss, and that I missed her. Minn promptly replied, saying she missed me too. We began to correspond by mail, supplemented by phone calls. I asked Minn if she would welcome a visit from me, and when she said yes, I booked a flight to Belgium. Though I'd had many conversations with Minn since my childhood, I had never thanked her for saving my life. This time I intended to do that.

As the airplane slowed down for its descent into Brussels, I watched the Belgian countryside approaching below. The airplane glided smoothly through blue sky over rectangular fields in which spring crops were beginning to grow in various shades of green and yellow next to the occasional rectangle of brown earth. I could see tiny white squares of farmhouses and farm buildings interspersed among the fields and connected by narrow ribbons of roadway.

As the airplane continued its descent, I had a sudden flashback to my time in Baudour during the war. More grey than blue then, the Belgian sky during the day was filled with hundreds of grey warplanes flown by British and American pilots heading east toward their targets. They were so high from the ground they looked tiny, like small mosquitoes. A faint but steady buzzing sound came from all those airplanes, all travelling at the same speed. When I looked up, I had the impression of a gigantic tapestry dotted with tiny war machines moving in lockstep toward their mission. A few puffs of white smoke appeared between some of the airplanes, possibly rockets exploding from anti-aircraft guns on the ground. None of them reached their target.

Now, during the airplane's descent, I felt a sense of the miraculous at how, many decades after that monstrous war, I was in the same area but on a very different mission. I saw and felt the total absence of the explosions of war. Below was a quilt of green, crops sprouting peacefully, waiting for summer. I was in awe at seeing those living colours from the comfort of my airplane seat — the colours of new growth somehow hinted at what world peace might look like. I sometimes had similar feelings when walking along a footpath in the woods of Algonquin Provincial Park, an oasis of forests, lakes and rivers, and walking trails, about a three-hour car ride north of Toronto. On those paths, I enjoyed bending down for a close-up view of soft green moss anchored to hard rocks or pausing to gaze at a patch of pastel-coloured flowers as white butterflies wove and flit among them. Now, as I was looking down at a panorama of fields from the airplane, something happened. It was as if whatever distance separated me from the earth seemed to magically disappear, and for a few moments, I felt completely at one with the flourishing, alive green below.

I stayed with Minn in her luxurious two-storey villa. She was frail and lived there with the assistance of caregivers who prepared meals and tended to her garden. We went on one outing together, to Brussels' central square, where I marvelled at the buildings, including the Town Hall, which was what remained of the city's Gothic architecture from the fifteenth century. At an opportune time during the week-long visit, I turned to Minn and thanked her for saving my life. Minn grinned, her eyes widening in happiness and also in surprise: "No need to thank me. You were a little boy. It was the right thing to do! Anyway, I knew all along you were thankful." And with that, she let me know that was all she had to say on the topic. It was a good visit, and I was glad I had expressed my gratitude. Minn died shortly after my visit, in 2001.

~

Each of those who rescued people from genocide has a different, heroic and sometimes tragic story. Yet what they had in common were their personal values and sufficient empathy to muster the courage needed to resist injustice. They took action at great personal risk, within the constraints of cruel military invasion, armed occupation, repression, loud explosions and murder. Their courageous actions saved lives, including my own.

I nominated Frantz and Minn to have their names inscribed as "Righteous Among the Nations," to receive recognition by Jerusalem's Yad Vashem, the World Holocaust Remembrance Center. My nomination was accepted, and the award was given in 2001 in Brussels where our daughter Mira had travelled to eulogize Minn.

Similarly, I honour the many individuals and groups, some well known, others not, who today are resisting injustices, near and far. Their courageous actions are harnessing an empathy toward victims and survivors of violence, dispossession, racism and genocide. They are growing a multitude of activist seeds that will blossom into mighty potential, saving lives, building our future. We all need to honour them, support them and join their resistance.

A Moment of Remembering

In 2013, my friend Yisrael Elliot Cohen sent me a memoir he had come across while working at Hebrew University. It was by Belgian historian Marcel Liebman, and it documents how his Jewish family members in Belgium were on the run and in hiding, desperate to avoid capture by their Nazi pursuers. Elliot noticed that some pages were about a man by the name of Karniol — no first name. According to the memoir, Karniol was a good friend of Marcel Liebman's father. As I read those few pages, I noticed details that seemed to fit: Karniol had come to Brussels from Czechoslovakia, was married, lived frugally with his wife and child, barely managing to pay the rent and gave his child into the care of non-Jews. I became convinced that this Karniol was indeed my father.

Liebman recounts that when Nazi troops captured my mother at our Brussels apartment, my father was not there. When he found out that she had been taken to a Nazi prison, my father decided to give himself up and join her. On his way to the prison, he visited his Jewish friends to say goodbye. It was Saturday, and he was invited to join them for their Shabbat lunch. Marcel Liebman was a witness to my father's last hours of freedom. He wrote:

He had lunch with us and, to our great surprise, seemed almost happy. We had a lump in our throats when he first arrived, but his composure spread to us too.

The meal was nearly over and the time for his departure approached. Once again, the tension mounted. Then Karniol, who had had a very un-Jewish childhood and had discovered the ancestral customs and rituals only when he got to know us, took advantage of a pause in the conversation to begin chanting "Vetaër libenou [Vetaher libenu]," the chant that belongs both to the Jewish liturgy and folklore. We joined in, our voices strangely steady. I can see him now, rising to his feet just as the canticle finished, going up to each of us and embracing us one by one, full of serenity. With his suitcase in one hand, he waved to us with the other, a big friendly wave. Smiling, he disappeared in search of his wife.

Both of them died in the camps.[1]

Reading about my father's serenity troubled me deeply. On the one hand, I felt happy for him, knowing that his love for my mother was so strong that he was willing to take a high-risk gamble to try to be reunited with her. On the other hand, with the benefit of hindsight, and knowing about the horrific, antisemitic hatred and cruelty of the Nazi police, soldiers and administrators, I am certain they would never have allowed such a reunion. He would have had no choice but to follow their arbitrary orders. I recently learned from archival documents that my parents were sent to Auschwitz from the transit camp Mechelen, or Malines, on the same day, October 31, 1942, but on different transports, my father on transport XVII, prisoner 869, and my mother on transport XVI, prisoner 154.

In the mid-1980s, my friend Morton Rappaport had helped me find information about what happened to my father. He told me that my father's registration number in Auschwitz was 72360. The fact that he was given a number indicates that he was not sent to

---

1 Marcel Liebman, *Born Jewish: A Childhood in Occupied Europe*, trans. Liz Heron (London: Verso, 2005). Originally published as *Né juif: Une enfance juive pendant la guerre* (Paris: Éditions Duculot, 1977), 84. Reproduced with permission of the Licensor through PLSclear.

the gas chamber immediately after arriving at Auschwitz. Knowing this, I can imagine the many ways that my father found his serenity collapsing when faced with sullen Nazi enforcers, with their scowls and their menacing weapons in hand, ordering him where to stand, where to wait, where to walk, which boxcar to enter for the traumatic, days-long rail passage to Auschwitz. I can imagine how he and other Jews barely survived in the overcrowded, locked and guarded boxcar, without food or toilets, dehumanized captives who were treated like cattle as they were transported to their bleak destination.

Decolonizing Social Work Education

As I moved toward making peace with my past and finding meaning in my social work practice, I began to focus more on deepening my knowledge in the field of social work education. My involvement in social work education began when I was hired by the University of Calgary as a teacher of social work. A few years later, I was elected to the board of directors of the Canadian Association of Schools of Social Work (CASSW), later renamed the Canadian Association for Social Work Education (CASWE). In the early 1990s, I attended one of their conferences at the University of Victoria, in British Columbia, which had a big impact on my future. The conference included a session with an Indigenous Elder Barbara Riley; her Indigenous name was Waubauno Kwe. She had set the chairs in a circle for about twelve of us who attended. She welcomed us and then lit a small amount of sage in a smudge bowl. As the gentle, sweet fragrance of sage permeated the room, Barbara explained that in her culture, smudging is used to open our minds and hearts to our spiritual selves. She then told us her story, how she came from Walpole Island (located near Windsor, Ontario), and how as a young adult she was attracted to the glitter and glamour of Detroit's nightclub scene, how her alcoholism almost killed her and how she turned her life around.

Barbara and I talked as we walked on the campus in Victoria along paths bordered by lush plants and a gorgeous landscape of flowering bushes. She told me about her courses at Laurentian University. I told her that I had been active with the social work educators' organization and had supported academics and students who were advocating for anti-racist social work education. This advocacy work was led by Dorothy Moore from the Maritime School of Social Work. Dorothy was a strong supporter of anti-racism and Indigenous rights. Barbara felt that Dorothy and I could support her interest in reaching out to Indigenous social work educators from other parts of Canada. After meeting Barbara at that conference, she and I stayed in touch and had numerous conversations about her life and mine. Barbara and Dorothy also became part of the social work educators' board of directors.

I felt my students could benefit from Barbara's teachings, so I invited her to attend my classes at Ryerson University. (In 2022, the university changed its name because Egerton Ryerson was a major architect of the brutal Indian Residential School System; it is now Toronto Metropolitan University.) She taught my students the Indigenous four-directional wheel consisting of the spiritual, emotional, intellectual and physical dimensions of human development, which she then personalized to her life. Barbara was articulate, funny and blunt. She criticized university education as narrow, attending exclusively to the intellect at the exclusion of the other three dimensions. She described most professors as acting as if they consisted only of their heads and two small feet, giving their teaching a very lopsided focus.

Aside from sharing Indigenous knowledge with my students, Barbara introduced an Indigenous way of teaching-learning. In all the classes she attended, she rearranged the chairs in a circle, sometimes with a smaller circle within the larger circle. She explained that when the teacher-Elder was speaking and introducing a topic, no one was to interrupt. This was to show respect. When she, as teacher-Elder, passed her eagle feather to the next person, it was that person's turn to speak. After completing their turn, the person was to pass the feather to the next person, and so on around the circle. No one was to interrupt the person holding the feather, also a sign of respect.

Barbara explained that the person receiving the feather was welcome to speak or could choose to be silent. That choice was also a sign of respect. The intention was to help each participant find their voice at their own pace. She asked everyone to refrain from taking notes: this was to teach the skill of active listening. Holding an eagle feather was intended to promote honesty and courage among each of the participants.

She pointed out that the purpose of this circle format was to encourage all participants to share their thoughts, feelings and spirit about whatever the topic was. She asked that what was shared in the circle remain in the circle: this was to guard against gossiping outside of the circle and to teach confidentiality. As a result, the learning was personal, full of sharing from the heart, often emotional with a spiritual dimension. The classes were fascinating, as participants reached for deeper meaning in their learning.

Students loved Barbara's teachings and her teaching style. They asked me: Why had our school not used this teaching method before? How come there were no Indigenous faculty teaching at our school? When could Barbara return to teach again? By then, Barbara and I had become friends. I felt honoured when she asked me to be her assistant in conducting a smudge ceremony at the start of the numerous classes that she was invited to teach at Ryerson. My role was to carry the smudge bowl from person to person, starting with Barbara. This way, students could quietly observe the motions that she used as she cupped her hand over the smoking sage and moved the smoke over her head, eyes, mouth, ears, then her arms, heart, stomach and legs while giving short explanations for these motions. When everyone had their turn, I would offer the smudge bowl to Barbara, who would hold it while I smudged myself.

Around that time, there was a social work faculty meeting at Ryerson, where I suggested that our school develop a required course to address Indigenous realities, to be taught by an Indigenous person. My suggestion was debated, voted on and roundly defeated. Other faculty members were annoyed with me: Why give priority to Indigenous issues? There were other more important topics, such as poverty, they argued. This showed me that opposition to being more inclusive was coming directly from my colleagues, leaving me feeling isolated from them.

Throughout this period, I felt supported by Monica McKay of the Nisga'a First Nation in British Columbia. For many years, she had coordinated Ryerson's Aboriginal Student Services. She was tactful, gentle, polite and tenaciously persistent in advocating for Indigenous students and for the hiring of more Indigenous professors. Several faculty members had recently retired, and the School of Social Work had hired new, younger faculty who supported my advocacy for curriculum changes.

Meanwhile, Barbara and I followed up on our conversations at CASSW. We teamed up at the national level with Indigenous social work educators to advocate for greater Indigenous content as part of new accreditation standards for all schools of social work across the country. This initiative was then carried forward by a new Indigenous caucus consisting entirely of Indigenous educators.

At Barbara's suggestion, we formed an Aboriginal Advisory Council to be a part of the Ryerson School of Social Work. The Council included an Indigenous Elder from the Toronto area, several Indigenous social workers from communities near the university campus and a few faculty members, including me, a new school director and the associate director. The Council made a unanimous recommendation to the school: it was time to hire its first Indigenous professor, which our school did, followed by other Indigenous hires who taught courses focused on Indigenous realities. My inner life felt hopeful. I could see my workplace taking constructive steps toward respecting Indigenous culture.

My role with the CASSW was largely supported by other social work educators. I had been active on its committees and elected to its board of directors and was also elected as its president. But there was one incident that occurred while I was at CASSW that made me realize how much the events of my childhood still affected me. It was a time when some members of the board of directors resented my advocacy for Indigenous Peoples to have a stronger voice in the association. An accusation was made against me that I had authored and sent an anonymous note disparaging the work of the association. Some board members questioned my integrity and called on me to resign as president.

Fortunately, I had a skilled lawyer who was outraged by the false accusation against me. This lawyer had observed and approved of my advocacy work at my university. A meeting was scheduled with the association's board of directors to clear the air. But that meeting turned out to be a personal disaster for me. I heard untrue accusations against me, and before I could defend myself, some board members resigned. Those resignations triggered a deeply hidden emotion within my inner life. Though I had not been conscious of it, I was carrying a suppressed feeling of having been abandoned by my parents as a child. Rationally I knew that my parents had not abandoned me — on the contrary, they did everything to save my life. But to my child self, who did not understand the looming genocide, my parents had abandoned me. I wanted to be with them, and they were no longer with me. These feelings were so painful that they were buried until triggered by these board members resigning.

The emotional echo of abandonment caused me to lose my balance at that board meeting. To my surprise and utter embarrassment, I wept in front of the remaining board members. My tears were misinterpreted by some as proving my "guilt" to the false accusation. As a result, more board members resigned, which further affirmed my sense of abandonment.

Though I knew the accusations against me were false, this episode did cause me to seriously question my ability to explain myself. The board members who refused to resign were Indigenous. Amid this organizational turmoil and further calls for my resignation, the national Indigenous caucus of social work educators issued a strong appeal for me to stay on as president.

My lawyer sprang into action. He wrote a scathing letter to all the resigning board members, excoriating them for irresponsibly absconding from their organizational responsibilities. The lawyer's fierce response also came to the attention of all deans and directors of Canadian schools of social work. Right after the lawyer's letter went out, I sent my own letter, accepting the resignation of the departing board members. I immediately invited other social work educators I knew, such as my anti-racist colleague, Dorothy Moore, to join the board. With a quorum now on the board, we could make decisions and plan the next annual meeting, where we would have an election.

At the annual meeting, a new board was elected, resulting in some staff leaving the association. The newly elected board members and other colleagues were very supportive of me, which enabled me to serve as past president for the usual term. At the same time, I quietly licked my emotional wounds while actively engaging my inner life to start the process of healing from my abandonment issues. Along with my self-talk, I was also doing God-talk. I felt God's reassurance that I was not alone. I asked God to offer me healing from the pain of being falsely accused. I asked God to help me dismantle the psychological triggers for feeling abandoned. I also thanked God for Rhona, who never wavered in her trust in me. I thanked God for the lawyer's dramatic defence of my behaviour. I also felt grateful to all those who had supported me during this rough passage. Gradually, I felt my balance returning.

Several years later, I was nominated for the association's highest award — an honorary life membership in the association for "distinguished contributions to social work education in Canada." Though I did not seek this award, I certainly welcomed the endorsement; it helped me feel vindicated. Nevertheless, I had also learned some hard lessons about how organizational infighting can rupture relationships, and I came to accept the gullibility of some people I had once respected.

At the time, the law required university teachers to retire at the age of sixty-five. As 2002 approached, when I would be required to retire after thirty years of teaching in Toronto, I wondered what I should be doing next. An answer flew in the day after I retired.

Expanding the Circle

As I was trying to figure out what to do after retiring from full-time teaching, Susan Silver, the director of the School of Social Work at Ryerson, told me that she had a suggestion from Jim Albert, an Indigenous Elder active at the national level with CASWE who was now a program Elder with First Nations Technical Institute (FNTI). He had asked our school director if she would appoint me as program coordinator for a new social work partnership that FNTI wanted to develop with Ryerson. She was happy to make that appointment and asked me if I was interested. When I replied with an enthusiastic yes, she set about making it happen.

As program coordinator, I consulted with FNTI about hiring teachers, recruiting Indigenous students and ensuring that students met the requirement for obtaining their social work degree. Jim was very helpful in orienting me to my role. He had been the director of the School of Social Work at Carleton University and had experience in meeting with senior university administrators. He welcomed me to tag along as he met with Ryerson's senior officials in order to shape this partnership. Jim also mentored me so that I would become comfortable teaching Indigenous students in the new program.

Jim remained program Elder for three years, after which FNTI invited Banakonda Kennedy-Kish (Bell) to assume that responsibility.

Her Indigenous name is Awnjibinayseekwe, and she is from the Bear Clan and third-degree Midewiwin, born on the outskirts of Sault Ste. Marie, Ontario. Banakonda is Anishinaabe with Irish ancestry and she has worked and taught extensively within Indigenous communities over decades.

When Banakonda began her stint as Elder, she and I had discussed her goal to introduce land-based education to the Indigenous students in our program. Instead of teaching in university classrooms, we would teach on the land, offering the equivalent of one course credit for each week-long program, or culture camp. We stayed in tents and experienced an Indigenous fast for twenty-four hours, while observing and appreciating the life of the grass, bushes, trees, air and water, all linked to the land. We built a healing lodge under the direction of the esteemed Elder of the Elders, Jim Dumont, an Ojibway-Anishinaabe of the Marten Clan and originally from the Shawanaga First Nation on Eastern Georgian Bay; Jim was Chief of the Eastern Doorway of the Three Fires Midewiwin Lodge. With him, we created structural supports from young saplings, covering them with a tarp and bringing in large boulders, which were heated and then had water poured over them to create steam and raise the temperature. We learned to apply teachings about addressing the trauma of genocide against Indigenous Peoples with the guidance of experienced Indigenous Elders, Knowledge Keepers and other cultural leaders. We learned about different medicines contained in the plants and vegetation around us and about Indigenous history and folklore as told through the stories and Oral Traditions of different First Nations.

In 2008, we scheduled a culture camp at Tyendinaga Mohawk Territory, near the north shore of the St. Lawrence River near Belleville, Ontario, home of FNTI. I was met at a railway station by Banakonda, who drove me to our campsite, where about thirty Indigenous students from all over Ontario were gathering. My previous experience camping had been with Rhona and my daughters about twenty-five years earlier, when we had used an army-surplus tent made of heavy burlap. Since that time, tents had become much lighter, with poles fitting into the various flaps so that they could be set up within minutes, if you knew what you were doing. The first time I tried to set up a tent at a culture camp, Banakonda howled with laughter as she saw me tangled up with poles that I had put into the wrong loops, and she helped to disentangle me from my mistakes. But on this occasion, I was grateful to find that Banakonda spared me the hassle of fumbling with tent poles and had kindly set up a tent for me before I arrived. She had even put a heater in it. Now we had time to briefly discuss some of the program that we had planned for the first day.

While on the land, students learned about Indigenous culture from Banakonda and other highly experienced Indigenous experts, such as Jim Dumont. Two highly regarded Indigenous scholars also joined our culture camp team of instructors: Dan Longboat and Bob (Robert) Antone. Dan was from the Turtle Clan of the Mohawk Nation members of the Haudenosaunee Confederacy; he was also the founding director of Trent University's Indigenous Environmental Studies and Sciences program. Bob was a member of the Turtle Clan of the Oneida Nation of the Thames; he was executive director of the Indigenous healing lodge, Kiikeewanniikaan in Muncey, Ontario.

Banakonda made it clear that this land-based education was not merely about having a good camping experience. Rather, it was meant to anchor the experience of students within Indigenous cultural teachings by Indigenous Elders and other Knowledge Keepers. Banakonda introduced an Indigenous perspective this way in a chapter that we co-wrote for a book about spirituality and social work:

Spirit comes first. This conception is the central determining, guiding force and influence in my culture. Spirit is the centre, the creative force, source, cause of energy and motion. Spirit and Creation are so closely connected they cannot be considered separately.... It is through the eastern door that we enter this life. This is the beginning of our journey as Spirits in physical form.[1]

That first night, as we got comfortable in our individual tents, I heard the joyful singing of Indigenous songs from students who were joining their voices together from different tents, one song after another, the singing getting slowly softer as I drifted off to sleep.

The next morning, before our first class, students and instructors walked to a large white canvas teepee that had been set up nearby. We took our places inside the teepee, sitting in a circle on cushions and blankets that we placed on the cold, grassy ground. A student had kindled a few logs, which were now burning at the centre of our teepee, warming us while sending smoke up and out through an opening at the top. The canvas door was wide open, letting the light from the morning sun stream in.

The few conversations among us stopped when Banakonda, who was sitting between the slow-burning logs and the teepee's doorway, held up a small pitcher of water and said a prayer in her Indigenous language. She then demonstrated an Anishinaabe water ceremony and talked about the many ways that water sustains our lives, noting that we all grow in the water of our mother's womb. She warned that clean water was being endangered by irresponsible human behaviour and that in traditional Anishinaabe culture, women were the protectors of the water.

After her teachings, students participated in the ceremony, which included passing the small pitcher of water to each person in the teepee. One of the students began to cry when she held the pitcher. The

---

1 Banakonda Kennedy-Kish (Bell) and Ben Carniol, "Vision and Belief within Indigenous and Jewish Spirituality," in *Spirituality and Social Justice: Spirit in the Political Quest for a Just World,* eds. Norma Jean Profitt and Cyndy Baskin (Toronto: Canadian Scholars, 2019), 66–67.

rest of us remained quiet. After her tears stopped, she told us that she felt awful because here was a beautiful teaching from her own community, but she did not know anything about it. How come no one had taught it to her until today? Banakonda pointed out that for years these teachings and ceremonies had been outlawed by the colonizers. It was not the fault of the student, her family or her community. We could thank the Elders who had kept these traditions alive by hiding them so they could now be passed down through the generations.

The next morning, we again met in the teepee, and Banakonda encouraged students to take turns guiding the water ceremony as a good practice and way to keep the teachings alive. The student who had cried the previous day said, "I'll do it," and we all listened as the student gave the water teachings. She spoke about what water meant to her, her voice shaky at first but gradually becoming more confident. She was finding her way to affirm her culture. I was moved by how, instead of feeling the shame induced by settlers, this student was feeling a fresh sense of hope, celebration and pride in the wisdom of her community's teachings. At that moment, I felt we were all kindred spirits in that teepee. I could now better understand what cultural revitalization looked like and could easily imagine this experience being multiplied over and over again.

~

One morning in 2014, while we were teaching on Tyendinaga territory, Banakonda and I were meeting over breakfast when we saw a news report on the television. Journalists were reporting that two groups of Tyendinaga activists were threatening to block freight and passenger trains heading west from Montreal and passing through Tyendinaga Mohawk Territory. The protesters were joining Indigenous communities from coast to coast that had, for years, been pressuring the federal government to launch a national public inquiry into missing and murdered Indigenous women and girls.

Our students let us know that they wanted to support the

Tyendinaga activists, and so Banakonda and I changed our teaching topic for that day and shared highlights from our experiences about how to stay safe in nonviolent protests. After the morning class, Banakonda and I quickly organized carpools and drove to the site of the protest, which was a rural road that crossed the rail tracks about fifteen minutes away. When we arrived, we saw a large fire on the road about twenty yards away from the tracks. The fire had been built by young Tyendinaga activists. They had parked a pick-up truck on which they erected a huge sign: "National Public Inquiry Into Missing and Murdered Indigenous Women and Girls." Police were present down the road, as were the media.

In this tense atmosphere, Banakonda and I were able to guide our students to offer nonviolent and respectful support to the activists. Students had brought their hand drums and proceeded to drum and sing honour songs to thank the demonstrators for continuing to draw attention to the need for such a public inquiry. One of our students was interviewed by the media, and we all cheered when we heard that student's name come up in favourable media coverage.

The second activist group from Tyendinaga consisted of women who wanted to speak with the media, but they had never done this before: they were nervous. With the reporter patiently waiting, Banakonda and I provided on-the-spot coaching to two of the women until they were confident enough to go on the air. Banakonda and I stepped back, and we heard the two activists give brilliant replies to the reporter.

The federal government did respond to the pressure, setting up this inquiry within the next year, to begin its work in 2016. The inquiry completed its work in 2019; it concluded that Canada continues to engage in a genocide against Indigenous Peoples.

Today, I still reflect on the depth and scope of Banakonda's teachings, which had an effect on both my Jewish spirituality and my identity as someone living in Canada: I had a growing awareness that I was part of a settler population. Learning about an Indigenous view of the all-encompassing Spirit, I could not help but reflect on my own spirituality. I did not fully understand why, but when I began discussing my Jewish spirituality with Indigenous students and teachers, I felt very comfortable. Perhaps it was because I was not trying to prove that my way was the best way. On the contrary, I recognized that mine was only one among many ways of understanding Spirit. I respected what I was hearing from Indigenous voices, which was different from a Jewish approach. I may have been influenced by my adoptive mother, Greta Cohen, who had said something when I was a young adult that stuck with me: "There are many pathways to understanding God, and we must respect them all." When I heard Indigenous Elder Jim Dumont say, "There are many different creation stories, and they are all true," he seemed to be echoing what I had heard many years earlier from my adoptive mother. I felt that though he was using different words, they were both saying that there are different pathways to reach an understanding of the sacred and that we should respect all of them without being judgmental or criticizing any of them.

As I learned more about how Christian missionaries sought to undermine the distinct Indigenous framing of spirituality, I came to understand the violence of colonialism and was hearing a new meaning for the word "settlers." This new meaning was expressed by Indigenous Elders, youths, activists, leaders, scholars and teachers. These Indigenous voices were saying that both the early settlers and the contemporary non-Indigenous population of Canada were all "settlers" because they were doing the same thing: occupying traditional Indigenous land and erasing Indigenous culture.

I understood that contemporary racism, combined with contamination of the land, unsafe drinking water and many years of underfunding basic services were encouraging Indigenous Peoples to leave their land to seek a better life in urban locations. The migration by Indigenous Peoples out of their traditional territories was accompanied by a flood of new developments on Indigenous territories: bigger hydro dams, along with new logging roads and wider highways that were supporting an expansion of oil, gas, timber, mining and other extractive industries. Aside from these industries taking over Indigenous land, their leaky pipelines and heavy tanker traffic were also environmental disasters waiting to happen.

These realities were unsettling. For many decades, I had used terms such as "mainstream society," to refer to non-Indigenous people and our institutions. In doing so, I had also accepted a prevailing narrative that ignored the theft of land and the destruction of Indigenous communities. In other words, I had been complicit with settlers in denying a history of the massive dispossession and harm that had impacted Indigenous Nations. As I became more aware of this meaning of "settler" in my later years, I felt a growing inner tension about this newly emerging part of my identity. I did not want to deny, reject, excuse or explain it away; I wanted to let this new understanding of my identity slowly percolate throughout my being.

What may also have helped me to accept this new awareness was reading the doctoral dissertation of an Indigenous scholar, Ruth Koleszar-Green,[2] which explores the idea that by being a settler, I was also a *guest* who had choices about how to behave personally and politically on this land that Indigenous Peoples called Turtle Island. I wondered if viewing myself as a settler-guest could offer me a pathway for evolving mutual respect between myself, as a non-Indigenous guest, and the Indigenous hosts of this land. Might such a pathway be welcomed by other settlers as well in order to build a better future between Indigenous and non-Indigenous people?

---

2 Ruth Koleszar-Green, "Understanding Your Education: Onkwehonwe and Guests Responsibilities to Peace, Friendship and Mutual Respect" (PhD diss., OISE/University of Toronto, 2016).

Threats to Empathy

After the National Inquiry into Missing and Murdered Indigenous Women and Girls declared its findings about the genocide of Indigenous Peoples, some Canadian leaders and media pundits objected. "Genocide in Canada? That's not who we are!" They argued that "genocide" was the wrong term. This response raised questions for me: Why was it that some people recognized the genocide against Indigenous Peoples, while others refused? The question led to others: Why did some Jewish Holocaust survivors and post-Holocaust Jews care about other people's suffering, while others did not? In fact, why should anyone care about the suffering of others? And unless people cared, was it even possible to prevent more genocide?

As I grew older, I witnessed the consequences of racism, and these questions became central to my inner life. In Cleveland, I had seen many examples of anti-Black racism. Then in Calgary and in Toronto, after retiring from full-time teaching, my work with Indigenous students provided many opportunities for me to witness anti-Indigenous racism that was driven by European colonialism. From my own experience, I knew about the consequences of anti-Jewish racism. My awareness of my personal history provided me with pathways to reach out to Indigenous students dealing with the intergenerational trauma created by being displaced from their home territories and cultural traditions and languages.

While seeking to develop supportive relationships with my students, I met Vivian Timmins, an Indigenous woman from the Cree Nation. I became familiar with her excruciating story because after she graduated, she was documenting her experiences and asked me if I would help edit her writing. She had found a publisher in Kentucky who would publish stories documenting the experiences of Indigenous women. I worked with Vivian, and her writing was published as a chapter in *First Lady Nation: Stories by Aboriginal Women*.[1] Through this process, I became familiar with both the trauma and the healing that she had experienced, and I got to meet her husband, who had helped her heal. Vivian was one of thousands of Indigenous children forced into a Canadian residential school and had been sent to one of these schools when she was just four years old.

This relationship helped me better understand not only the trauma that Indigenous Peoples have suffered at the hands of settlers, but also how Indigenous Peoples have learned to grow and thrive. As I made an effort to understand the absence of empathy by settlers toward Indigenous Peoples who were suffering from addiction or struggling with extreme poverty, my inner life was able to identify a gigantic barrier blocking many people from feeling empathy. That barrier, I realized, consisted of massive blame machines that are designed to trigger our prejudices. When it comes to Indigenous Peoples, I could identify numerous negative stereotypes within the vast warehouses of anti-Indigenous prejudices. We became so busy blaming, shaming and dehumanizing Indigenous governance, practices, communities, families and individuals that we prevented ourselves from feeling any empathy.

---

1 Vivian Timmins, "Honouring My Spirit," in *First Lady Nation: Stories by Aboriginal Women*, vol. 3, ed. Linda Ellis Eastman (Prospect, KY: Professional Woman Publishing, 2015), 88–101.

Such blame machines are not restricted to powerful prejudices against Indigenous Peoples. Just as those who had gained handsome material benefits and huge privilege from the theft of land and the destruction of Indigenous culture directed blame against Indigenous Peoples, so too those who had forced Africans into slavery required a strong blame machine to avoid facing how they had financially benefitted from the cruelty of imprisoning slaves on White-owned plantations. My inner life was appalled by how many massive blame machines targeted other populations: Arabs, Jews, Muslims, Roma, Asians, followers of Bahá'í and other groups, who are then blamed for being outcasts. These different blame machines extinguished the humanity of their target groups, leading to a lack of empathy, racist persecution and genocide.

But instead of acknowledging these racist blame machines, we hear benign words from glib politicians who reinforce the image of Canada as a tolerant society and who talk at length about Canada "being on track" to reduce whatever injustices exist. Prime Minister Justin Trudeau has said more than once that his priority is to move forward on all the ninety-four Calls to Action made by Canada's Truth and Reconciliation Commission. But he has not yet taken tangible steps to respond to Call to Action #47, which addressed the Doctrine of Discovery and *terra nullius*.

The Doctrine of Discovery was applied by European colonial nations when their sailboats "discovered" the Americas and denied Indigenous Peoples any legal rights to sovereignty over their territories. This racist denial was based on the principle of *terra nullius*, which viewed Indigenous territories as "empty" because they were occupied by non-Christians. I was appalled to learn how this principle had been carried out during the European Age of Discovery, when Christian explorers were able to claim lands for their monarchs so that they could exploit the land, regardless of the original inhabitants. The Assembly of First Nations in 2018 noted that the Doctrine of Discovery was premised on the "racial superiority" of European Christian peoples to dehumanize, exploit and subjugate Indigenous Peoples, and therefore was "the very foundation of genocide" against Indigenous Peoples.[2]

On March 30, 2023, the Catholic Church via a Vatican press statement finally repudiated the Doctrine of Discovery.[3] By contrast, Prime Minister Trudeau has failed to follow up on the Canadian government's explicit repudiation of the Doctrine of Discovery with concrete action. Until that happens, Canadian courts will continue to be influenced by this Doctrine with reference to property rights and Crown land, continuing to undermine Indigenous claims to title over their traditional territories.

Learning about this wasn't impersonal research for me. Being keenly aware of the pain, suffering, violence, trauma and massive loss of life caused by the genocide of my community, I needed to proceed carefully. In my experience, I knew that protesting against injustice allowed me to act on my empathy. And so I joined a street rally in Toronto on February 17, 2020, to be with others offering support for the railway blockades by Indigenous land defenders in different parts of Canada. It was a lively, well-attended rally, with myriads of signs proclaiming solidarity with Indigenous land defenders. We shouted chants in support of Wet'suwet'en Hereditary Chiefs in Northern British Columbia, who were blocking a gas pipeline from passing through their territory. The rally was followed by a march across Toronto's main streets, led by a spirited group of Indigenous youth.

This demonstration brought home to me that underneath this conflict, there was also a deep clash of ideologies. On the one hand, the Canadian economy and its business leaders wanted to deliver our

---

2 Assembly of First Nations, *Dismantling the Doctrine of Discovery*, January 2018, 2.
3 Nicole Winfield, "Vatican Formally Renounces Discovery Doctrine after Decades of Indigenous Demands," *Global News*, March 30, 2023, https://globalnews.ca/news/9589418/vatican-renounces-discovery-doctrine/.

natural resources to market. On the other hand, Indigenous leaders and their supporters felt that Indigenous sovereignty and environmental protection needed to limit the capitalist exploitation of gas, oil and related resources.

On more than one occasion, Banakonda explained to me why she was opposed to the term "natural resources." She warned that when parts of nature are treated as objects, to be owned, this leads to unlimited exploitative taking from nature, putting our very survival into question. As she wrote in *Case Critical: Social Services and Social Justice in Canada,* a book that we collaborated on: "The work ahead of us, I believe, is the untangling of ourselves, each other, and our communities from consumerism, from materialism and the abuse of land, water, and life. We are all caught up in this unsustainable taking."[4]

Banakonda was challenging a basic premise of capitalism. Agribusiness, mining, fishing-boat factories, timber and fossil fuel industries: they were all dependent on exploiting nature for profit. Tension grew within my inner life as my own loyalty to capitalism was challenged. I knew that, for years, I had conformed to contemporary narratives, practices and laws that expected my unquestioning loyalty to capitalism.

Banakonda Kennedy-Kish (Bell), Raven Sinclair, Ben Carniol and Donna Baines, *Case Critical: Social Services and Social Justice in Canada*, 7th ed. (Toronto: Between the Lines, 2017), 193.

Calls to Action

As I reflected on various forms of racism, as well as on World War II and my own experiences with genocide and anti-Jewish racism, I wondered, Had our history taught us anything? I was beginning to believe there was at least one lesson from all the bloodshed, suffering and violent upheavals of the twentieth century: all dictatorships and their extremist ideologies are social poisons that start by creating gigantic, unstoppable blame machines to kill empathy, and end up killing millions of innocent people. Watching world events, I ask myself: Will we allow the huge blame machines to steamroll over our lives and the lives of our children and grandchildren? Will we remain bystanders, in fear of today's tyrants and dictators? Or will we resist? We need bold action.

In recent years, I have witnessed the Israel-Palestine conflict becoming more steeply polarized, as different religious extremists and their leaders have become the enablers in escalating this conflict. From the Jewish side, I know that many lovers of Torah understand that the teachings from the Jewish Bible must never be used to harm people. There is a gentleness that pervades the practice and study of Judaism, which is reflected in warm family ties and strong community relationships. At the same time, my inner life has become uneasy about a screechy, explosive reality that makes me concerned for the present and for the future. It has been painful for me to realize that some lovers of Torah want to assert their beliefs by lashing out at others through hate and violence. My inner life became agitated when, in 1995, many Jewish Orthodox communities condemned any Jewish leader who was willing to negotiate with Palestinians for a two-state solution. Tragically, that frenzied agitation by right-wing Jews against other Jews operated under a horrid illusion: that God opposed any Palestinian state on territory that was under Israel's military occupation. At the time, Israel's Prime Minister Yitzhak Rabin was willing to negotiate a two-state solution. As a result, he was murdered by an Orthodox Jew.

This tragic murder created a new normal, where the relations between Israelis and Palestinians became fraught by violence from both sides. With plenty of religious extremists, bigots and other fanatics inside all the parties to this conflict, their appeal to religious texts set the whole region aflame. Military security against terrorist aggression became Israel's top priority, and Israel developed lightning strategies to wage war. This was comforting to many Jews, including me. But it left another question: Where are Israel's mighty strategies for peace? I have been closely following developments in Israel as well as visiting the country for years, and it is my observation that Israel has no government-financed institutions dedicated to peace that are equivalent to its capacity to wage war.

What has injected hope into my inner life are the many organizations that bring together Israelis and Palestinians — men and women who have laid down their weapons and rejected all violence and who are engaging in nonviolent activism, offering alternatives to violence. The message of these organizations is hopeful, and sharply contrasted with the prevailing pessimism due to the escalation of military power and domination. The Israeli government is now, in 2023, trying to overhaul the judiciary, limit the power of the courts and give more control over law-making and public policy to the government. But fortunately hundreds of thousands of protesters in Israel and outside of Israel are courageously taking a stand for democracy and for minority and human rights, to uphold the vision contained in Israel's

Declaration of Independence that the State of Israel "will ensure complete equality of social and political rights to all its inhabitants irrespective of religion, race or sex."[1]

Yet, despite these hopeful movements, I believe my pessimism about the immediate future is well founded. Most countries have a bias toward the mobilization of violence, with little or no institutions to promote peace. My inner life bursts with questions: Why do countries choose military power? And where will this lead us? In a world overloaded with nuclear weaponry, my imagination points to answers. I imagine fierce, thunderous explosions from nuclear rockets followed by forests of tall mushroom clouds rising, wiping out one city after another, obliterating one nation after another, threatening all human life on Earth.

We may not like it, but we are all interdependent. The violence of war-making, especially with nuclear weapons, will kill all of us. It is horrific that each superpower today develops new generations of nuclear weaponry to create worse and more lethal destruction. Today, there are about two thousand nuclear weapons on high-alert status throughout the world, ready to be launched within minutes of a warning. This is the folly we must stop.

Within my lifetime, I remember the disturbing spectacle of the Soviet Union and the United States arrogantly escalating their nuclear arms race, openly insulting each other and boasting about their capacity to annihilate each other. On the heels of the massive anti-war movement that ended the American military involvement in the Vietnam War, there arose a gigantic worldwide anti-nuclear, peace movement. Rhona and I joined it, along with thousands upon thousands of other Canadians. We marched on Toronto's main streets with our two young daughters as part of a huge and growing movement. We

---

[1] The full text of the declaration in translation is available at https://main.knesset.gov.il/en/about/pages/declaration.aspx.

even formed a Jewish group that we called Shalom Disarmament. We held periodic planning meetings at Toronto's Holy Blossom Temple, developed educational programs and leafleted Jewish venues. Along with countless other groups, we warned about the existential dangers of the runaway nuclear arms race. As peace activists from other countries joined together, this international peace movement grew strong enough to cause some government leaders to dismantle their doomsday scenarios. That was then. It worked before, and I want to believe it can work again.

The United Nations has been useless in blocking the invasion of Ukraine led by Russia's president and ruthless dictator Vladimir Putin. One way to resist escalation of war is to abolish the United Nations Security Council and its dysfunctional veto power. We need bold action to create a new General Assembly mandated to enact laws that criminalize any nation invading another and to outlaw any nation from inciting to destroy another nation. We need a new General Assembly to create new laws to criminalize the promotion, production, distribution and deployment of weapons of mass destruction. We need world leaders to create an entirely new international court of criminal justice that would have automatic jurisdiction over any individual from any nation whose hands are dripping with the blood of their war crimes. The General Assembly needs to initiate new laws of universal jurisdiction for courts and universal authorization for police from any country to apprehend a war criminal from any nation, to be brought to the new international criminal court to face charges. Only bold actions will block the ominous threats to bankrupt the limited democracy that has evolved in Canada and elsewhere.

As I leave these pages, I acknowledge that there are no guarantees that we will succeed in overcoming these dire threats to our future. Indeed, we may lose the battle to avoid climate catastrophes, to prevent a nuclear World War III and to protect our democracy. Many people have suggested that it will take miracles to protect our future. That is why I believe we must consider: How do miracles happen?

Miracles

Despite my experiences with loss and war, and despite logical projections into a future that causes many to despair, my hope has remained strong. I am convinced that the emergence of human life is an amazing miracle, just as the emergence of a seed is a miracle, just as surviving genocide is a miracle. Our challenge is to align ourselves with an appreciation of the miracles all around us on a daily basis: the sun rising in the morning — we awake, we breathe, we sense familiar surroundings. We have the capacity for empathy, and for the courage to seek justice, to speak truth to power and to know that love can trump fear, shame, blame and anger — to find goodness when the odds seem impossible.

It is miraculous how seasons flow into each other and how the leaves in autumn change from green to spectacular orange, red and yellow, then fall from their branches, shrivel up and die. Just as it is miraculous that previously powerful empires and their pompous leaders sooner or later enter the dustbins of history. Autocratic, narcissistic tyrants, intoxicated with their oversized egos, ruthless in their cruel aggression — they too shrivel up and die. May we witness many such miracles in our day.

Biblical insights into spirituality were miraculous, as is the drying up of old perceptions — that racism, aggression, greed and violence are "just part of human nature." Like dying leaves, these outmoded perceptions of human nature are making room for new attitudes to miraculously grow and evolve so that we can reframe human nature, motivating our respect for all life.

Human agency and the spirit of God can be found in most miracles. For settler populations to stop harmful extraction activities within Indigenous territories and to stop racist colonialism against Indigenous culture, we need to have a prior miracle — the disconnection of politicians from their subservience to the dirty money of those who promote the endless expansion of fossil fuel projects and nuclear arms industries. Such miracles could rescue democracy from hypocritical politicians who feign support for social justice while winking at their public administration to embolden the ultra-rich, entrenching their lust for wealth. While we may be aware that such miracles will be necessary, we may not realize it will be up to you and me and many, many others to do our part, with help from God, to bring them about.

Long before I became an adult, the love I received from my original parents strengthened my ability to enter another world, another religion, while receiving the care and affection of my rescuers who miraculously shielded me from the Nazi genocide against Jews. When I was reunited with my family in Ottawa, and returned to my Jewish roots, it was the special, miraculous love that I received from my maternal grandmother that enabled me as a teenager and young adult to deal with the aftershocks of violent trauma from war and genocide.

Meeting with Indigenous Elders who were social work educators in Victoria, British Columbia, and in Toronto, Tyendinaga and Kitchener, challenged me to deepen my listening, my empathy and to grow my relational capacities gradually, miraculously, into a respectful settler-guest who supports Indigenous governance, human rights and land-back negotiations. Such a role welcomed me to Wilfrid Laurier University's Faculty of Social Work, where I teamed up as co-author and co-activist in solidarity with Indigenous social work scholars such as Kathy Absolon, Gus Hill, Lori Hill, Timothy Leduc and wise Indigenous Elders, such as Banakonda. The ways Banakonda has helped students in social programs address the traumas they encounter as helpers in their communities provides an amazing holistic, spiritual model. She draws upon the resilience and wisdom of Indigenous culture, centring the importance of Spirit. Her humility and courage miraculously spoke to my soul.

These encounters helped me to continue grieving the murder of my parents and of the six million innocent ones who were the victims of the Nazi genocide against Jews. It was as if I had found a spiritual oasis that was supportive and healing and that allowed me to feel my parents' love in a new, vibrant way. I am grateful for God's role in that miracle, which supported my healing journey away from fear, shame and feeling abandoned.

It is also miraculous to share my story with you, the reader, while I find meaning in this process of recollection and reflection. I do have a regret — that many people who would appreciate reading this story are no longer here. My original parents, my adoptive mother and adoptive siblings have all passed away. Rhona's brother, her parents and their siblings are all gone. My rescuers and their immediate families are gone. My Baudour friends, gone. My Ottawa friends have either drifted away or passed on.

As we grow older, it is a common experience that people we cared about have left or are in the process of leaving us. How do we continue to live without them? Much will depend on the lens through which we see life and death. If we adhere to competitive, rugged individualism as our lens, we may feel arrogantly superior in being the last one standing. Or we may become bitter and resentful, feeling abandoned by everyone else. Or we may become obsessed by self-pity, as if we no longer mattered. All these harmful feelings may be miraculously replaced by intentionally reframing our lens to appreciate the many gifts bestowed on us through the grace of a forever Spirit. A sense of such miracles can enhance our capacity for humility, for gratitude and especially for empathy toward other lives as we circumvent the contempt instilled by the dictates of our mammoth blame machines.

If we are lucky enough to have benefitted from new family members, including grandchildren, we may feel less alone as we grow older. If we have made new deep friendships, we can miraculously share our life journey while still living within this physical realm. I feel fortunate that Rhona, my life partner of over fifty years, is still with me. We still very much care about each other — a real blessing. If we are also spiritual, we have another dimension to access: experiencing the presence of the souls of people we cared about who have left this physical realm.

I am grateful for our human capacity to enter into a diversity of spiritual journeys. God, Spirit, Allah, Jesus, Buddha, and other spiritual and theological entities are shaped by different historical experiences and sacred traditions. Different does not mean better or worse; we must respect them all. If some are drenched with the blood and indictment of their cruelty against others, they must address their crimes, through remorse, restitution, compensation and honest repentance — the miracle of transformation in partnership with God. Sacred perspectives are different, but I believe they share a common celebration of life and an awe of its amazing mystery. I believe that beyond or inside this mystery, there is a miraculous infinite Caring that transcends difference, rooted to an eternal sense of sanctity that facilitates vision, empathy, relationships and knowledge to inspire our motivation for carrying out sacred acts of courage toward justice.

This book is intended to add one more voice toward our survival and a thriving future. If my experiences, plus the efforts of many others, can build on our resilience, our empathy, our courage and our social activism to bring about justice, then let's not wait. Let's each of us resolve to take action today, joining with others in social movements and goals we share, to seek justice — and with God's help — to create the miracles we need to safeguard our future.

Correspondence

This section includes some correspondence between members of Ben's family and his Belgian rescuers, Minn and Frantz Vandenheuvel, as the war in Europe was ending and in the immediate postwar period. The letters, originally written in German and French, have been translated and edited for brevity and consistency of style.

From Julius Gerstl to Madame Vandenheuvel
May 2, 1945
Happy to know Beni is with you and we pray you refuse any organization wanting to take him [illegible] and cable us we appreciate you infinitely best regards grandparents.
 Julius Gerstl

From Grete [Greta] Cohen to the Vandenheuvels
March 17, 1945

My dear Mrs. Vandenheuvel, my joy was great today to receive your kind card to tell us of the well-being of our beloved little Beni for whose well-being as well as his parents we worried so much these last 2–3 years! Beni's mother, Mrs. Elsa Carniol, is my youngest sister, and my parents as well as I only pray that we may hear soon from her and her husband! I only know of Beni through my dear parents whom we brought to Canada just before the fall of Czecho-Slovakia, and Beni was born at my parents' home. We all love the child deeply and thank you from the bottom of our hearts for your kindness to that child.

Now, my dear Mme Vandenheuvel, what can I do for you and Beni? I would gladly send what you need. One can send 4-pound parcels from here. How is the food situation or clothing? Is any organization as perhaps the "Joint Distribution" or "The Friends" (Quakers) looking after the care and need of these many children whose parents were taken away? We were talking and praying daily for the safety of my beloved sisters and their families. My other sister and her family escaped fortunately last October to Switzerland from Budapest. One Aunt formerly of Berlin died in Shanghai. I am married [illegible] in this grand Canada for over 21 years, but my days are dark since I lost my dear husband last fall. My oldest son serving in the Canadian air force got his discharge recently to help me in business, which I have to carry on since my husband died. Yes, we all suffered so [dreadfully and] deeply, and it is only the hope to see their beloved ones again that keeps my dear parents going. Your dear card was a sunray for us. We read here so often of grand people as you are from letters and reports our boys who serve over there write about. May God bless you and reward you. I shall ask someone to add a few words in French to our beloved Beni. Do you think there could be a possibility for Beni to come here? Is there any organization who arranges such cases? By the way, how did you have my address? I shall send today also a parcel with a few eatables. Again my thousandfold thanks and appreciation for your kindness.

Most sincerely,
Grete Cohen

From Julius and Fanny Gerstl to the Vandenheuvels
May 24, 1945
My dear, good Madame Vandenheuvel! Dear Verschueren family!
We are very happy to have received a letter today from our cousin Sgt. Walter Kohner, dated April 28, in which he tells us about his visit to you.

Walter informs us that our little Beni, praise God, is the picture of good health, which of course we owe only to your exceptional kindheartedness and self-sacrifice. He cannot say enough to us about your extraordinary kindness, delicacy and sensitivity, and about the great love with which you all surround our little Beni. But also, of course, about the love that little Beni has for all of you.

Unfortunately, at the moment we are not adequately able to express to you, dear Verschueren family and Madame Vandenheuvel, the extent of our great debt and gratitude. We can only ask God to bless you all for the good deeds you have done.

Walter also writes to us of the great misfortunes you all suffered at the hands of the Nazi beasts, who so mistreated your dear Mr. Vandenheuvel and sent him to Germany. We pray to the Lord daily that Mr. Vandenheuvel as well as our dear children Elsa and Mathias Carniol may return home as soon as possible in good health.

Walter Kohner also sent us some photos of you and little Beni and will soon send us the latest pictures. We find the photos all very beautiful and are really happy with them, and praise God, we also see that little Beni is very handsome and well developed.

Hopefully by now you have already received some of the small packages we and our daughter Grete Cohen sent? Unfortunately, from Canada you are only allowed to send 4 pounds 6 ounces. We are at a loss as to what to do to solve the question of clothes for Beni, which are certainly a necessity. We hope that these postal regulations will be changed soon after the war in Europe is over, and then we will send everything necessary with the first post.

We ask you, dear Madame Vandenheuvel, to keep little Beni with you, because we hope that his parents will soon return with God's help and that they will be able to take care of him themselves, or that we or our daughter will be able to take this great care from you.

Dear all, please accept once again our heartfelt thanks for your angelic kindness and for all the good and beautiful things you have done for our children and our sweet little Beni. Please tell little Beni often about his good parents, and about us, his grandparents who love him very much, and about his Aunt Ida and Aunt Grete.

Many millions of kisses to little Beni, and also many greetings to all of you,
    Gratefully yours,
    Julius and Fanny Gerstl
    P.S. I ask you to keep little Beni with you for the time being, and not to hand him over to anyone or any aid organization.

From Grete Cohen to Mrs. Vandenheuvel
September 20, 1945
My dear Mrs. Vandenheuvel,
Your kind letter addressed to my parents arrived here some time ago. We want to thank you sincerely. We are delighted to hear that your dear husband arrived safely home, and may God bless you with the best of happiness, above all good health and that no more sorrow may come to you. We also were very happy to read darling Beni's letter, which someone translated for us. We admire how lovely [you can write in English], dear Mrs. Vandenheuvel. My parents would have answered you long ago, but they only understand German and a bit

[of the] Czech language. They get along quite alright with English now since they are here, but not good enough to write letters. Since about 6 weeks my parents live with me here in Ottawa and it is not so lonesome for me. We all are so grieved not to have any sign or news of our beloved Carniols; it is really heartbreaking. What a blessing it was for little Beni to have had the privilege to find such fine noble friends as you are. It is such a satisfaction for us to know that Beni is happy and well taken care of. We know it'll be some time yet before we shall be able to have Beni, as soldiers and other important officials are only allowed to cross the ocean. But we are not worried and are contented that Beni is happy with having his uncle Frantz at home. Well, I shall close now, with the kindest greetings from my parents, children and myself.

Yours appreciatively,
Grete Cohen

From Julius and Fanny Gerstl to the Vandenheuvels
November 1, 1945
My dear Mr. and Mrs. Vandenheuvel!
On October 20, we received your dear, detailed letter of September 20, and we are very happy to know that you both are healthy, as well as our dear little Beni.

We read all your news with great interest, and we are glad that Mr. Vandenheuvel is healthy again and has made a full recovery.

We thank you a thousand times for the beautiful picture of our little Beni, which made us very happy, and we are happy to know that the child is well cared for and well looked after in such a good family.

We are trying very hard to get little Beni to us as soon as possible, but our children in Switzerland would very much like to take little Beni with them to Palestine, if possible.

We are very sad and desperate to still have received no sign of life from our dear children the Carniols, and we pray daily to the good Lord to help them and for us to receive good news soon.

Dear Mr. and Mrs. Vandenheuvel, we are in great debt to you for your great help and love to our dear little Beni, and we pray to God to bless you both and all your dear family. We promise that when little Beni is no longer with you, we will be grateful to you for the great debt we owe to you, and of course we will continue to send you parcels.

Unfortunately, we can only write in German, but you can write in French or English; we have friends who will translate your beautiful letters for us. Do you have the possibility to get our German letters translated over there?

Two weeks ago, I was in Toronto, and our friend Mrs. Waldman, who read your dear letter, promised me to write to you in French. Did you receive the letter in French from her? Hopefully the candies came in time for little Beni's birthday?

A good friend of ours, Music Professor Percival Price from America, will soon be travelling to Europe, and he wants to visit you and little Beni, which would make us very happy.

For today, the warmest greetings to both of you, to your dear parents the Verschuerens, and to all your dear relatives, and to our dear little Beni a million hearty kisses, from both of us and our dear daughter, Grete Cohen.

Gratefully yours,
Julius and Fanny Gerstl

\<handwritten note\>
My dear Vandenheuvel family and my sweet little Beni! Please accept the most heartfelt thanks from me as well for your so loving and nurturing friendship to our dear grandchild little Beni, which you showed also to our dear children the Carniols.

May God bless you for it!

Many, many warm greetings to all of you, and a kiss to our sweet little Beni in spirit.

I remain your grateful Fanny Gerstl

From Julius and Fanny Gerstl to the Vandenheuvels
January 12, 1946
My dear Mrs. and Mr. Vandenheuvel!
Please excuse me greatly for writing in German, but unfortunately my daughter is not home today and so I have no one to write in English or French. First of all, our most heartfelt thanks to you for your rare, great kindness and the love with which both of you and your dear family surround our dear little Beni.

May the good Lord bless you all and reward your noble deeds and human kindness with health and the best well-being. We also thank you very much for your kind letters and New Year's wishes, and we hope that you also received our good wishes and New Year's package.

On New Year's Eve, Beni's uncle, Fred Carniol, one of the brothers of our dear Mathias Carniol, who lives in Brooklyn, New York, came to visit us with his wife. He has sent the shoes and linen for little Beni, and he will now try to get a permit for Beni to go to New York, from where it will be easier to bring the child to us.

We know very well, dear Mdm. and Mr. Vandenheuvel, that little Beni could not be in better hands anywhere in the world than he is with you, and we also know that it will be difficult for you, dear friends, to part with the child, but unfortunately, it has to happen one day. We owe you a great debt of gratitude, and may God reward you with his blessings for your good, noble hearts.

We and our daughter Mrs. Cohen were very pleased with little Beni's letters. Unfortunately, we do not have a new picture of us, and so we are sending you an older one from 1939. Of course, we have all grown much older since then, as a result of our great sorrows and heartache.

We hope to receive good news from all of you soon and send our warmest greetings to you, and also to dear Mr. and Mrs. Verschueren and your dear brother and sister-in-law.

Yours gratefully, and with much appreciation,

Julius Gerstl, Fanny Gerstl, Grete Cohen

My dear little Beni!

We were very pleased with your dear, beautiful letter, and also with your New Year's card. We are happy to know that you are healthy and well. Mr. Cousin (*sic*.) Sonenschein has written to us many nice, good things about you. Keep being good! Respect, appreciate and love good Mdm. and Mr. Vandenheuvel, they are your best uncle and aunt, good-hearted people.

Study well, pay attention in school, and take good care so that the teacher will also be happy with you.

We greet you and kiss you a million times, your loving Grandfather and Grandmother, and your Aunt and cousins Eddie, Sidney and Erica

P.S. 3 international reply coupons and 1 photo enclosed

From Julius and Fanny Gerstl to the Vandenheuvels
March 30, 1946

My dear Mrs. and Mr. Vandenheuvel!

Please excuse us, dear friends, for writing again today in German, but unfortunately, we old folks can manage neither French nor English.

To our regret, we have had no direct news from you and little Beni since December, but we hope that you all are healthy, including your dear parents the Verschuerens, and your brother and sister-in-law.

Our friend Lieutenant Colonel Professor Price has written to us twice with a wonderful report about his visit to you, as did our friends Walter Kohner and Artur Sonenschein earlier. All of them were very complimentary and impressed with you and your whole family and little Beni. Our dear friend Prof. Price also told us about the lovely trip to Antwerp.

We have not heard from Mr. Carniol from Brooklyn about the permit for Beni to go to America, and unfortunately there is no possibility of emigration to Canada at present. Our dear daughter Ida Fekete in Hotel Hoheneck, Engelberg, Switzerland, who has a permit to Australia, would like to take Beni with her, but unfortunately that is also now impossible. And so, dear friends, you must be so kind and good as to make the great sacrifice of keeping Beni with you in your good care until one of these matters is settled.

May the good Lord reward you all, dear friends, for your noble hearts, your great help to your fellow man, and all the pains you have taken; may he keep you all healthy and give you the happiness you deserve.

The sad and terrible news about our dear Elsa and Mathias Carniol is so awful that we are losing our nerves and health and can hardly bear it. May the good Lord help us!

Hopefully there is someone in Baudour or Brussels who can translate our letter to you? Hopefully Beni is reasonably well-behaved, studious and obedient? We are very anxious about the child and are longing for him.

In the hopes that this letter finds you all in the best of health, we greet you all, including your dear parents the Verschuerens, your brother, sister-in-law and Beni, with our warmest thanks.

Yours very appreciatively,

Julius and Fanny Gerstl. Best greetings also from our daughter Grete Cohen.

<handwritten note>
Dear Mr. and Mrs. Vandenheuvel!
Please accept from me especially warm greetings and sincerest thanks for all the great kindness and love with which you surround our little Beni.

I will take the liberty of enclosing in the next package a small memento intended for our dear Elsa, namely a gold necklace with a medallion and little Beni's picture in it, and we hope that it will bring you a little joy. We hope to receive a letter from you soon. Greetings to you and your loved ones, with much love, your Fanny Gerstl

P.S. 3 return coupons for the reply are enclosed.

From Julius and Fanny Gerstl and Grete Cohen to the Vandenheuvels
May 21, 1946
My dear Mdm. Vandenheuvel!
Having received your dear letter of May 7, we are very sorry to learn that Mr. Vandenheuvel is unfortunately ill, and that our Beni, too, had to suffer through that well-known childhood illness. We can therefore very well understand that you found no peace and no time to write letters.

We hope and wish from the bottom of our hearts that Mr. Vandenheuvel will soon recover fully in Switzerland and will return to you in good health. If it is possible for him to visit our children in Zurich, they would be delighted to have him.

Our dear friend Prof. Price returned a few days ago from his great journey and brought us greetings from you and Beni, which we return most cordially. Prof. Price told us many sweet and lovely things about you and your whole dear family, and also about our little Beni.

Unfortunately we also have sad news to share with you. Mr. Fred Carniol, Beni's uncle in Brooklyn, New York, died suddenly of a heart attack, at the young age of about 45 years, a very fine and good man. This tragic loss of course also complicates the matter of Beni's permit, because the widow's future does not seem to be secured.

We must therefore ask you, dear Mdm. Vandenheuvel, to keep Beni with you for a while longer under your good care and supervision, until our efforts succeed in obtaining for him a permit for Canada, which will take some time.

Professor Price also mentioned to us that perhaps you, dear Mdm. and Mr. Vandenheuvel, would move to Canada. It goes without saying that in this case, as soon as the emigration laws are changed, we would gladly do everything we can to make it possible for you both to come here.

With the sincere wish that this letter may find all of you and Beni in the best of health and well-being, we send the warmest greetings to both of you, as well as your good, dear parents the Verschuerens and your dear brother, his wife and children, and millions of kisses to our Beni.

Yours gratefully,

Julius and Fanny Gerstl and Grete Cohen

My dear Beni! We were very, very pleased with the lines you wrote to us. Stay healthy and study well, and we are looking forward to hugging you soon in Ottawa, Canada, with many kisses from us and Aunt Grete, and from your cousins, Eddie, Sidney and Erica Cohen, Grandpa, Grandma and Aunt Grete

From Ida Fekete to Mrs. Vandenheuvel
June 3, 1946
Dear Mrs. Vandenheuvel!
If I am writing to you for the first time today, dear Mrs. Vandenheuvel, it is not because I have not found the time to do so before now, but only because I lacked the necessary tranquility. Please know that I have great respect for you, that in my eyes you are something quite extraordinary, something special and noble. I can't find the right words to tell you how I feel about you and that alone kept me from writing to you. I owe you so much thanks! The word "thanks" is much too small to express what we, my family, owe you and your dear husband. You took Beni into your home without knowing that you would have to protect and take care of the child for several years. And all our friends, without exception, cannot tell us and my dear parents enough about how well Beni is doing in your care, how attached you and your dear husband are to him and he to you. How happy

this knowledge makes us only we can measure, who have already lived through so many terrible things. Three and a half years ago, when I received the devastating news from a gentleman unknown to me, named Sinkovits, that my good, beloved sister and brother-in-law had been deported, I was so broken that the world died for me. He did not mention Beni, but I still knew from my beloved sister herself that she had placed him somewhere in the countryside with distinguished people, a young couple. She wrote to us that I should never ask after the child, they would tell us about him themselves. Later she also wrote that her brother-in-law had visited the child and found him with nice, round cheeks, and how happy she was about it! The next message was from Mr. Sinkovits, and since then I have been waiting daily for a sign of life from my good sister Elsa.

When I received the terrible news, I completely withdrew from the outside world. I stopped going out. We lived in our villa on the most beautiful square in Budapest and had a friend from my youth, an emigrant from Teplitz-Schönau, staying with us as a guest for half a year. She always tried to console me, saying that she had lost her parents and four brothers and sisters, while I could still hope to see my sister and her husband again. Yes, I did hope, because otherwise I would not have been able to continue living. When the doorbell rang, I always ran to the door and hoped that it would be Elsa, and in the same way I waited for the mail to come. In winter, when the bell rang in the evening, I always imagined that it would be her, and then I would sit alone with her on the divan in the living room with the lights out, hugging her tightly as she told me everything. I couldn't sleep, I couldn't rest, and I felt sorry for my husband and my son. But I could not help it. My good mother-in-law was also living with us. I got along well with her, like with a close friend, and she also loved dear Elsa so much. She advised me to take up work with a charitable organization again, as I had done in the past. I used to work actively with a charity committee helping poor orphan children from Poland and Slovakia. These refugee children were sent to Palestine in groups.

So, I worked there with the committee from early in the morning until late at night, but my suffering did not diminish. Every hour I thought of her and where little Beni might be. We had no idea where to look for him and even if we had known, we would not have written to you, so as not to inconvenience you in any way. My thoughts were always with my sister and the child. Whether he might still be in the same place? Or whether he had to leave there as well? Whether he was healthy? I prayed every day for my beloved sister, brother-in-law and Beni and always prayed that God would also protect those who had taken Beni into their care. In the spring, I bought for my sister a dark blue dress, coat, hat, shoes, bag and gloves, all in blue with a wide collar, so that if she came to me with torn clothes, she would have something nice to wear. For Beni I also bought a nice knitted light blue suit, coat and hat, and shoes. And then some toys, so that when he came to me, he would find things to play with.

Then came May 10, 1944, when in a matter of 15 minutes we were put out into the street by the SS, without knowing where we would sleep that night. By then, it had been a year and a half since we'd heard from my sister Elsa. My first thought at that time was, how would Elsa's letters reach me now, since the SS had immediately moved into our apartment and occupied the rest of the house. I could no longer write to my dear parents either. After 6 weeks of moving from house to house, we ended up being sent to Bergen-Belsen. In a sealed cattle car we travelled through Germany for two weeks, and I always asked to look out of the barred windows, just in case I might see my sister somewhere. When we arrived in Bergen-Belsen, the first thing I did was to look through the windows of the other barracks to see if I could catch a glimpse of my beloved sister. It was impossible to ask any questions; the soldiers with their rifles at the ready ensured that no words were exchanged. But every day I hoped to catch sight of her somewhere.

Yet all my searching was in vain. I could only keep on praying that God would protect her. I longed to make it to freedom to continue the search for my good sister, her husband and child. There, where so many complaints were heard, not a single complaint came from my lips, only sighs of sorrow for my sister. I was dizzy with hunger, but I never complained. My husband, my boy and I would lie to one another, claiming that we weren't hungry in order to force a piece of bread on the others. We came to Switzerland and my first task was to look for dear Elsa, her husband and child. I silently hoped to hear some news of them through my parents and was again completely broken when I heard negative things. Wherever I went, in cities or small villages, I inquired about them, always looking in all the shops to find them. The last time I worked for a year and a half as a chef at a hotel that was set up as a refugee home for 120 people. I worked very hard for 12 to 14 hours non-stop, and even then, I never found out anything. Often, I felt as if I would collapse, and immediately I had to think of my good sister Elsa, and then I would feel better again.

My boy, 17 years old, attends school in Geneva, and we refugees get paid transportation every 6 weeks to visit our children, and every time I return, I hope to find a sign of life. Unfortunately, up until now, I have heard nothing from them. Still, I keep on hoping that it will come, because life without her would give me no support or substance. We always understood each other so well, in a way that was rare to see. Often, I think about whether you knew my sister for a long time, and then I say to myself that you surely must have, and that is why you are so good to Beni. Elsa couldn't help but be kind and helpful to everyone; she had nothing but joy to give, and everyone loved and appreciated her. She never tired of doing things to bring joy to others. She was my father's right hand – he had a big shop in Teplitz-Schönau, and she took care of her household, which was a joy to be in. How she looked after her husband and her son, and her greatest pleasure was to see them all happy. How devoted her cook and Beni's nurse were to her — for each of them she had just the right understanding! When she fled to Brussels, we asked her if she had registered with a refugee organization and her answer was, how could we even ask such a thing. As long as they still had some jewelry they could sell, they would not do such a thing — it would feel as though they were taking a piece of bread away from another refugee. It was the same even later, when things were already very tight for them. Once she wrote that all that remained of her whole fortune fit in one corner of a cupboard, but still she was not sad, because her sunshine Beni was with them. She hoped that things would get better again and that her husband would get back on his feet again; she had faith that God would help them. Only when her husband was taken away did she become sad, but when he came back, she wrote that she had no other wish than for all three of them to stay together. When I was still in Budapest, I always carried all our photos with me into the air-raid shelter, the way others took their jewelry with them. I also brought them all with me to Bergen-Belsen and was very happy to have them. But when the SS handed us over to Switzerland, they took all our photos and papers away from us at the border, and there were to be no exceptions and no pleading. My heart seemed to break as I watched them snatch away my precious pictures of my beloved Elsa and throw them in a pile with the others. Only two very small pictures were hidden as if by chance among other things, and together with a picture of Beni that my parents sent me thanks to your help, they always sit on my little table.

Dear Mrs. and Mr. Vandenheuvel, I know you have done so, so much for Beni — so much work, so much care, so much sacrifice and so much love given. My husband probably already wrote to you that we have the firm intention to take the child into our care, as soon as my husband has some firmer footing. I just want to assure you and your dear husband that we will never forget what you have done for the child and for our whole family. I will never stop telling Beni about your great selfless love for him, and I am convinced that the child will be bonded to you with great gratitude, and when he is grown up, he will always be aware of the debt he owes to you, dear Mrs. and Mr. Vandenheuvel. Until then, may the good Lord keep you healthy and take you both under his protection. With the illness of your dear husband, may the bad times be over for all of you, and I wish from the bottom of my heart that he may return home to you healthy and fully recovered. ...Now, unfortunately, Beni's uncle has also died, and this news has shaken me deeply. I don't know what to do now. Send him to Canada? I'm afraid that my good parents are already too old and too nervous to raise such a young child. And my sister Grete is in the shop all day. I'm not sure if you know the Schlossmann family. They were also in Brussels and were good friends of Elsa's husband and now live in New York. Mrs. Schlossmann wrote to me that they would like to take Beni in and that they would love and cherish him. I don't know the family myself, but my dear Elsa often mentioned them in her letters.

Now I have one request: could you and your dear husband send me a very small photo? I would like to see how our little Beni is doing, at least in this way.

For Beni, I am enclosing two photos of us, which I had taken on the occasion of my dear Mama's birthday, and my smile was for her benefit. Because deep inside me everything looks quite sad and gloomy.

Please forgive me for writing so much to you today, but I couldn't help it, I had to tell you all this. Please stroke little Beni's hair and kiss him for me, and tell him that we all love him very much and that later he will come to us in Australia. Hopefully the package with Paul's outgrown clothes and a small doily for you, dear Mrs. Vandenheuvel, has arrived by now. Today I'm sending a chocolate bar, which is now permitted. With best regards, I remain your grateful Ida Fekete

From the Gerstls to the Vandenheuvels
January 29, 1947
My dear Madame and Monsieur Vandenheuvel!
My Dear Friend! My Dear Beni!

We were very pleased with your dear letter of 14 January, although we regret very much that you, dear Madame Vandenheuvel, were ill and not feeling well. But we hope that with God's help you are well again, and we wish good health to you and Monsieur Vandenheuvel, your dear parents the Verschuerens, and your whole family, and especially our dear Beni.

We were very happy to get your New Year's telegram and wish you all a happy New Year 1947 once again.

Our Beni should study very diligently in school because in Canada, the schools are very strict, and the children all have to be very attentive, good students. So, dear Beni, you are such a good, obedient dear child, and you will make your aunt, uncle, and us happy by studying hard!

We will write to America this week, and order 600 cigarettes for you. Unfortunately, it usually takes 2 months for them to reach you there. Our children's journey from Marseille to Australia will also take almost 2 months via the Suez Canal!

Perhaps you, dear Monsieur Vandenheuvel, will be lucky enough to find a job here in Canada, which would make us very happy. Unfortunately, however, the country of Canada is still very unfriendly to immigration, and we have not yet been able to get a permit for Beni, even though there is already a Canadian consulate open in Belgium. And so, dear friends, you will have to be patient with Beni and keep the child with you for the time being.

Your grateful, sincere friends,
The Gerstls

From the Gerstls to the Vandenheuvels
March 27, 1947
My dear Mr. and Mdm. Vandenheuvel!
We were very pleased with your dear letter of March 15, and are very

glad that you, my dear Mrs. Vandenheuvel, are, thank God, in better health again, and that Mr. Vandenheuvel and our little Beni are both healthy, praise God.

We are, as ever, very sorry that we unfortunately still have to write to you in the hated German language, and we can imagine how hard it must be to find someone to translate our letters, but unfortunately, we are too old to learn, and years of worry and sorrow have weakened our memory.

We are having an extremely cold winter here, like in Siberia, with lots of ice and snow since December. But in the house, it is nice and warm; we have oil heating. People here do a lot of winter sports, and the kids are all very hardy. We are glad that the warm leather skirt (*sic.*) fits Beni and keeps him warm. Hopefully the shoes, pants, sweaters, stockings, and socks sent for his birthday were also the right size?

My dear little Beni! We were very happy to hear from Prof. Price and Aunt Vandenheuvel that you are now studying well at school. Keep it up, because here in Canada all children have to study hard and be very attentive in school. We hope to have a lot of fun with you, and we are all looking forward to seeing you again soon.

With many warm greetings and kisses from all of us,
your Grand Pa and Grand Ma (*sic.*)

From Julius and Fanny Gerstl to the Vandenheuvels; handwritten note at bottom in English from Grete Cohen
July 15, 1947
My dear Mdm. and Msr. Vandenheuvel!
We thank you very much for your kind letter of 6 July and enclose the declarations signed at the Belgian Consulate by my daughter Mrs. Grete Cohen and myself. We also hope that the [Aide] aux Israélites [Victimes] de la Guerre, 41 Boulevard du Midi (Mrs. Renée Goldstuck and Mr. Guns Mansbach to be contacted in the reply), to whom we

have also written, will provide you and Beni with all the necessary help. As soon as we receive word from you that all documents are in order, we will immediately reserve a plane ticket for Beni. Please let us know as soon as possible by telegram, which we will of course pay for. We don't know yet if it is better for Beni to travel Brussels-New York-Ottawa or Brussels-Ghent-Ottawa?

We thank you from the bottom of our hearts for your great, kind efforts, and the kindness and love you have always shown to our Beni, and we send our best regards to you and your dear parents the Verschuerens, as well as to your dear brother, his wife and children. We send many kisses to Beni and are looking forward to his arrival here soon.

Yours,
Julius and Fanny Gerstl

<handwritten note in English>
My dear Mr. and Mrs. Vandenheuvel!
We just came from the Belgian Consulate and are enclosing the papers. As soon as we know that everything at your end is alright, we shall try to reserve a place for Beni's trip. Or it might be possible for you to do that. However it is convenient for you, we shall abide. Meanwhile, a thousand thanks for all your trouble, and any expense involved we shall be glad to reimburse you, of course. I do hope sincerely that your own affairs with regard to coming to Canada is taking its normal course and before long [you will] be able to come. Dearest Beni, we all are looking forward to having you here. Your cousin Erica is brushing up her French knowledge. But I am sure it will not be long and you will speak English, though we certainly will see to it that you shall never forget the beautiful French language.

Meanwhile, our most friendliest greetings to you all.
Sincerely,
Grete C.

From Ben to the Vandenheuvels
Undated
Dear Aunt Minn and Uncle Frantz,
I was unhappy to learn that you will not be back in time for my departure but that you will nevertheless be coming to join me in Canada in three months....

I would like to have the photo of monsieur le curé [the parish priest] and the Sister Superior. Also one of Raymond. Do not forget above all to send me my toys and a "chaplet" which I don't have.

I hope you are in good health and that your vacation went well and that you will return [illegible].

If all goes well and as soon as I will be in Canada, I will write you a letter telling you all the news and that I await with impatience TIN-TIN and your news.

I will never forget you because I love you very tenderly AND I will write you often.

Many kisses and soon,
Your little Beni

From Julius and Fanny Gerstl to the Vandenheuvels
Undated
My Dear Friend! Monsieur and Madame Verschueren! Monsieur and Madame Vandenheuvel!
We hope you received our telegram sent to Baudour and Brussels, about the happy and healthy arrival of our dear Beni, whom we find to be very handsome, praise God.

Besides God, we have you alone to thank, dear friends, for the child's safe arrival, but we also thank you from the bottom of our hearts for the great care and first-class attention you have given Beni for all these years. The child is very sweet and kind-hearted and has quickly settled in with us, but thinks and speaks of you all very often, with great love.

Beni and all of us will surely remember you all forever with great gratitude and love, and we will continue to send you updates about Beni from time to time.

Hopefully you will come to Canada soon? We don't know if the American Joint paid for the various stamps for the travel documents, or if you have had any expenses with these papers, but kindly let us know if you did.

In the next parcel we will enclose Ansco and Kodak colour film again; last week they were not available.

For today, much, much thanks from us once again, with the warmest greetings to you all.

Gratefully yours,

Julius and Fanny Gerstl

<from Ben, in French>
P.S. I went to the doctor for a check-up, and he said I was in perfect health, 100/100, thanks to your good care.

From Grete Cohen to the Verschuerens and Vandenheuvels
August 28, 1947
Family Verschueren – Vandenheuvel.
My dear friends,
Forgive me for addressing this letter to both of you, but I think both of your families — Vandenheuvel as well as Verschueren — were so responsible in the well-being of Beni that my heart dictates me to address you both. No doubt you received our cable of the safe arrival of the child. The excitement in our home before — especially from my parents — was great. There were great emotions in all of us when the plane alighted and at last we held Beni in our arms. It seems — despite language difficulties — we got along well immediately. My 3 children, Eddie 23, Sid 20, Erica 15, all have enough French knowledge to make Beni feel at ease. We all took Beni immediately

into our hearts. I suppose that was [natural]. He seemed very bright and well — though I understand he was a bit airsick over Ireland. To give him the proper start or be guided by his physical makeup, I took him yesterday to our house doctor. Though Beni is a bit small and underweight, the doctor found him in very good health, which made us very happy. Today Beni is already one of the children in the neighbourhood, rides his tricycle and is contented. His appetite is not big, and we are pleased to see that he is not keen on sweets. All in all we find Beni a very worthwhile person, and what I should have done in beginning this letter, I do now. To thank you for your kindness, your generosity and — last but not least — your intelligence to make Beni what he is. As you know, English is an adopted language for me, and though I speak it for 24 years, on occasions like this, words fail me. It is people like you who strengthen faith in humanity in those who went through a lot. We had [indescribable] losses and heartaches these last few years, but it is faith which keeps us one strong and going. People like you are the essence of life itself.

Don't think that your efforts on behalf of Beni are a thing of the past. His every action and word [reflects] the fine upbringing he was privileged to receive at your home. We shall always endeavour to keep his memory of all of you alive and never forget to talk to him of what you were and still are to him. We also realize that getting Beni ready involved lots of extra work, anxiety and expenses and therefore beg you please to give us the pleasure to reimburse you with all we can. I do know our debt to you cannot be paid with money, but nevertheless please do not hesitate and we shall gladly abide.

And now we hope it will not be long and we shall greet you my dear Mr. and Mrs. Vandenheuvel here in Canada. Please let us know if there is anything we can do for you. After all we live in the capital city, and sometimes a personal request is quicker looked after, than by letter.

We saw the lovely pictures of all your dear family and are greatly impressed with them. Each and all of you may have God's blessings. Enclosed I send you a picture which was carried in the local daily paper. As you see, Ottawa was quite excited over Beni's arrival.

Again, my and my family's sincerest and most heartfelt thanks for everything. We do hope to hear from you when time permits you. In sincerest friendship, I remain with friendly greetings to you all,
Grete Cohen

From Ben to the Vandenheuvels
Undated
Dear Aunt Minn and dear Uncle Frantz,
Thank you for the letter which you sent me and I was very happy to receive the magnificent map which you sent me. Today I am free and I have nothing to do therefore I said to myself that it would give you much pleasure to know about the life I have in Canada. I am going to tell you what happened at the beginning when I came, when I left Belgium. At my departure there was Parrain, Marraine, Aunt Yvonne, Uncle Maurice, Michel and Francine and I believe there also was Uncle Albert. I would have really wanted to see the plane before it took off but it was impossible since I was in it. I left Belgium I think it was on Sunday and I arrived in New York on Monday afternoon. A stewardess said, "You are the little passenger that someone is waiting for, isn't that so?" "Yes," said the other one. After that, they put me in a waiting room where I waited for 10 minutes, then someone came to find me, then someone walked a bit with me and finally I stood at the door where we were driving outside. I saw 3 or 4 aunts who began to question me: "Where are you going?" Another said, "How old are you?" Another, "Are you from Liège or from Brussels?" Another "It really is him!" And all this was in English. One of my cousins came with a car and we had a little tour of the city to show me what it was like and its skyscrapers are marvellous. My cousins took my aunt to the building where she lived. I stayed in the car with my cousin

George who drove the car. Then he went with me to the store where my Aunt [illegible] works and when she saw me she was happy like anything to see me.

My cousin, me, and my aunt went to a room in a hotel where he was staying. It was a skyscraper which was more than 23 floors high.

The next day I took a plane for Canada. The stewardess did not know how to speak French but she knew that there was a passenger who spoke French. Therefore I was seated next to him during the complete trip and he asked me if I wanted to be friends.

And when I arrived in Canada all my family was very happy to see me.

I will finish this letter by giving you many kisses,

Your Beni

From Julius Gerstl to the Vandenheuvels
November 5, 1947
My Dear Dr. Vandenheuvel and Mrs. Vandenheuvel!
We are very happy to have received your very dear letter from Halifax just 10 minutes ago, reporting your successful trip and safe arrival, which we are more than sincerely pleased about.

My wife, who is a very pious and godly woman, has been praying daily for your well-being, so that your plans and wishes may come true, and so we are now happy to know that you have landed safe and sound in Canada. May this beautiful country grant all your wishes and keep you both in good health.

Beni is at school at the moment, and we know how happy and delighted he will be when he comes home to find your dear letter and learn that you have both arrived in Halifax. Hopefully you have left your dear parents Mr. and Mdm. Verschueren and all your dear relatives in good health, but they must all be very anxious for you. Well, maybe they will also come to Canada later?

I don't know if you received our last letters and monthly parcels, which we have continued to send regularly, but hopefully you instructed the post office to have them sent to your dear parents. Beni is very good and brings us a lot of joy. He already understands a lot of English, but is slow to speak it, because our grandchildren here speak too much French with him. Beni is very popular here, all our family and friends love him very much.

With the wish that this letter finds you in the best of health and well-being, we will be glad to receive good news from you again soon. And in this expectation, we welcome you most warmly,

Your sincere friends

<handwritten note from Fanny>
My dear Mrs. Vandenheuvel and Dr. Vandenheuvel!
Beni just got home from school and added a few lines. He was so delighted to hear that you both have arrived here in Canada safe and sound and promised me he would reply to both your letters this afternoon after school, so hopefully he will keep his word. I also wish you the best of luck in your new home. You have been much in my thoughts, and I have been praying to God for your health and happiness. My daughter is coming back from Montreal tomorrow and then she will surely also write to you. Beni brings us much joy. He already understands a lot of English and is getting comfortable with speaking it. We hope to be able to greet you both soon in person, here in our own home.

I remain, with the highest esteem for you, your Fanny Gerstl

<handwritten note in French from Ben>
Aunt Minn and Uncle Frantz Thank you for the two letters you sent me reporting your good news. You'll get a long letter from me tomorrow or the next day.

Beni

From the Gerstls to the Vandenheuvels
November 10, 1947
My dear, dear Mrs. and Dr. Vandenheuvel!
From your detailed letter sent to our dear daughter Grete Cohen, the contents of which I unfortunately understand only in part, we learn to our great regret that the same great housing shortage exists in Halifax as here in Ottawa, and in fact everywhere in the world. Our dear children in Australia, who still live in a furnished room, and had to accommodate their only son outside the city, also have many complaints along these lines, and so we can understand only too well that you do not feel very comfortable in Halifax at present. But we hope that in time a suitable apartment will be found for you. Due to the continuous abrupt changes in the weather, our daughter has caught such a bad cold that she has had to stay in bed for a week with catarrh, and so I wanted to respond to your dear letter so as not to keep you waiting too long for an answer. Our daughter will also reply to you herself as soon as she feels better.

Today I want to reassure you that Beni is in good health, is a diligent student and already understands and speaks a lot of English. He was very, very pleased with your letter and beautiful birthday card and present, and he enjoys playing with the airplane a lot. It goes without saying that he thinks often and fondly of you both and of all his loved ones, for he is a clever, intelligent boy who understands very well how much gratitude he owes you for the infinitely great sacrifices you made over all the years he was in your care.

As for the question of further religious education, which you have touched upon, my dear friend, we have thought it best not to dwell on it too much for the time being, so as not to upset Beni's spiritual equilibrium.

As much as we understand that in Belgium and especially in the critical, dangerous time of the occupation and also later, it was not possible for you to do otherwise — in order to save Beni — than to let him take part in Catholic religious education, you will also understand, my dear friends, with the kindness of heart and intelligence that we know you to have, that now Beni, as a child of Jewish parents — his father was a leading figure in Zionism, and we ourselves, his grandparents and great-grandparents, aunts and cousins, have belonged to the Jewish faith since time immemorial — must raise the child again in the Jewish spirit and the Jewish religion.

How could it be possible, here where Beni lives with his grandparents, aunts, cousins and other relatives, seeing and hearing our Jewish ritual prayers and Jewish life every day at home, that he alone would lead another life belonging to another religion? We assure you that even where this is concerned, we practise the greatest tolerance imaginable, that we appreciate and respect Catholicism and other religions that worship a single God as we do. It also goes without saying that with regards to this question, we will, after some time and with the necessary sensitivity, come to an understanding with Beni without causing him pain or denigrating the Catholic religion in the slightest, since we also appreciate it, as already mentioned.

Ottawa is a capital city, but not a big city; there are three religious communities living here, and although we get along well, Catholics and Jews are still quite socially isolated, and it would be impossible here for Beni, living in a Jewish household with his Jewish grandparents, Jewish aunt and her children, to be brought up outside the Jewish tradition, without exposing himself to contempt from both the Jewish and the Christian side.

We hope and wish that you, our dear friends, whom we appreciate and admire so much and to whom we and Beni owe so much gratitude, will understand this honest and sincere statement and will not feel offended in your religious feelings and take us for ungrateful people.

But there is a divine prayer to which we must all bow and submit and respect, and so we hope that we will also find the necessary understanding among you, dear friends. We hope also that our daughter will write to you herself after her hopefully speedy recovery, before she takes a much-needed vacation to visit a sanatorium in the States for a few weeks.

It is clear that Beni thinks of you with great love and will never forget you as long as he lives, given his disposition and noble heart.

Hopefully you will receive good news from your dear parents and brothers and sisters in Belgium? We ask you to send them all greetings from us and from Beni as well. Hopefully the parcels and magazines we sent to Baudour, which left here on 19 September and 19 October, will arrive on time.

Continued on December 2: Unfortunately, due to my sudden cold and illness, this letter had to be set aside and could only be finished today. I hope that our daughter has perhaps already answered your letter? She was also ill and had to stay in bed. I recently turned 75 and have nevertheless recently had to look for a job, and so I have taken over an agency, visiting the local tailors with wool samples, to earn a little money. My dear wife will also soon be 75 years old and is busy in our small household; she and I occupy two small rooms in our daughter's house, which is unfortunately not too spacious. With the maid, there are 8 people living in the house. Beni sleeps with his older cousins in a room on the 3rd floor. He has a very good appetite and spends a lot of time outdoors.

Now we have a lot of snow and he plays with his friends in the open air, dressed very warmly. Unfortunately, he has one very bad trait: he is very lazy about writing, even though my wife has been nudging him gently and firmly every day to write you a nice letter thanking you for your dear letter, birthday card and present, he keeps putting it off from one day to the next, although he talks a lot about you and is thinking of you.

Due to illnesses on all fronts, our daughter has had to postpone her trip, but as soon as she feels better, she intends to leave in the next few days for the sanatorium, where she will probably stay for two weeks. In any case, we hope that you have received or will soon receive a letter from her.

For today, only the warmest greetings from both of us, and Beni, who sends you many kisses.
Your sincere and grateful friend,
Julius Gerstl

<handwritten note from Fanny>
My very dear friends,
Please excuse us for only now replying to your dear letter, as my husband and daughter have been ill. I wish you good luck and good health in your new homeland. We were very sorry that this letter had to sit unfinished for so long and could only go out today. I hope and wish you much luck and good health in your new homeland, which you will surely find here, with God's blessing. Beni is a good boy and now has private classes after school. He speaks a lot of English and already understands almost everything, but he will never forget the French language, which he loves, and which is much spoken in our house. He talks to me and my husband with great love for his Aunt Minn and Uncle Frantz. He is not spending Christmas with his Aunt Carniol, and we would be delighted to welcome you into our home. With this pleasant anticipation, I send my warmest greetings to you both,
Fanny Gerstl

Acknowledgements

I am grateful to the Azrieli Foundation's Holocaust Survivor Memoirs Program and to the managing editor, Arielle Berger, who warmly received my manuscript. My editor, Devora Levin, has provided exceptional editorial talent and sensitivity in addressing my traumatic experiences and in her notes and suggestions.

Yisrael Elliot Cohen provided very helpful edits to improve an early draft of this work. I am fortunate indeed to have such a good friend who is also a highly talented editor. He recently retired from employment in Jerusalem at Yad Vashem, the World Holocaust Remembrance Center and has extensive knowledge about Jewish history prior to, during and after the Holocaust.

I am also grateful to Beth McAuley, an experienced and excellent editor. With a keen eye for a potential book, she encouraged me to expand the pages of my initial manuscript and to improve its flow, pointing out where my voice had faded too far. She supported my advocacy for progressive change as an urgent theme of this book. I feel grateful for her help in strengthening my voice.

I'm grateful to my good friend, Lesley Simpson, who came up with *Hide and Seek* as the title and a theme for this book. She is also the successful author of *Yuvi's Candy Tree*, a children's book based on the true story of an Ethiopian youngster who tricked robbers in a dramatic exodus from Ethiopia.

Thank you also to writer Krista Foss, author of the acclaimed novel *Half Life,* who, with her experience in the world of commercial publishing, offered suggestions for ways my manuscript could be improved. I am grateful for Krista's non-directive suggestions that helped me invite readers to enter more deeply into my story.

In addition, I acknowledge the mentorship, teachings and friendship of Indigenous Elders, Aunties and Uncles who helped me to unlearn the colonial narratives that I was socialized into. Indigenous leaders also helped me appreciate the wisdom and spiritual insights of Indigenous culture. I am grateful to Elders and teachers: Waubauno Kwe (Barbara Riley), Mishike'n (Jim Albert), Awnjibinayseekwe (Banakonda Kennedy-Kish [Bell]) and Okimawininew (Joanne Dallaire).

I'm also grateful to Indigenous leaders: Monica McKay, Michelle Sutherland, Gus Hill, Lori Hill, Cindy Blackstock, Giselle Dias, Kathy Absolon, Tim Leduc, Raven Sinclair, Heather Green, Sarain Fox, Bonnie Freeman, Ruth Koleszar-Green, Katie McLellan, Raven Morand and Dan Longboat for their support.

My immediate family provided me with understanding, support and wonderful encouragement: Rhona, Mira, Naomi, Brian Gabor and my grandkids, Noah and Chloe, kept my spirit up. And of course, my wider family, including Brian Cohen, Mike Cohen, Steven Cohen, Susie Shosh Charendorf, Mike Cherney, Barbara Cohen, Roz and Gary Judd, Len Phillips, Chuck and Ruth Dixter.

My circles of friends, allies and supporters include Veronika Cohen, Becky Keshet, Marcia Beck, Jim and Kathy Chang, Jill and Morris Moscovitch, Leonard Molczadski, Cyndy Baskin, Sheri Weisberg and Brian Horychka, Hannah Fowlie, Stefan and Mary Krieger, Susan Silver, Jennifer Poole, Olga Palmateer, Sonia and Joel Kurtz, Dorothy and Cathryn Moore, Janet Horowitz and Sol Hermolin, Yaakov and Tzila Schneid, Anne Moorhouse, Hannah Brown, Elaine Cohen, Beth Porter, David Lesk, Ellen Katz and Jim McCall, Anne Clavir, Marcia Gilbert and Shalom Schachter, Miriam Bloom and Victor Rabinovitch.

My activist circles include Jessica Hutchison, Pam Chapman, Luisa Quarta, Judy Tsao and Steve Pizzano, Paul Agueci, Rhonda Teitel-Payne, James Kuhn, Jadie Schettino, Carolina Gana, Deborah Frenette, Elizabeth Radian, Frieda Forman, Sam Blatt, Ronnee Jaeger, Lev Jaeger and Shlomit Segal, Linda McQuaig, Donna Baines, and Lesley Turner.

My Jewish mentors and teachers include Rabbi Ed Elkin, Rabbi Joseph and Rachel Ben David, the late Stephen P. Cohen, Michal Erel, Ruth Rohn, Harry Fox and Tirza Meacham, Rabbi Edward Feld, and the late rabbis Jonathan Sacks and Abraham Joshua Heschel — all provided direct or indirect affirmation for this journey.

I am grateful to all of you, and to many others not listed here.

Glossary

Allied forces The coalition of countries that fought against the Axis powers (Germany, Italy and Japan, and later others). At the beginning of World War II in September 1939, the coalition included France, Poland and Britain. After Germany invaded the USSR in June 1941 and the United States entered the war following the bombing of Pearl Harbor by Japan on December 7, 1941, the main leaders of the Allied powers became Britain, the USSR and the United States. Other Allies included Canada, Australia, India, Greece, Mexico, Brazil, South Africa and China.

Auschwitz (German; in Polish, Oświęcim) A Nazi concentration camp complex in German-occupied Poland about 50 kilometres from Krakow, on the outskirts of the town of Oświęcim, built between 1940 and 1942. The largest camp complex established by the Nazis, Auschwitz contained three main camps: Auschwitz I, a concentration camp; Auschwitz II (Birkenau), a death camp that used gas chambers to commit mass murder; and Auschwitz III (also called Monowitz or Buna), which provided slave labour for an industrial complex. In 1942, the Nazis began to deport Jews from almost every country in Europe to Auschwitz-Birkenau, where they were selected for slave labour or for death in the gas chambers. In mid-January 1945, close to 60,000 inmates were sent on a death march, leaving behind only a few thousand inmates who were liberated by the Soviet army on January 27, 1945. It is estimated that 1.1 million people were murdered in Auschwitz, approximately 90 per cent of whom were Jewish; other victims included Polish prisoners, Roma and Soviet prisoners of war.

bar mitzvah (Hebrew; son of the commandment) The time when, in Jewish tradition, boys become religiously and morally responsible for their actions and are considered adults for the purpose of synagogue and other rituals. Traditionally this occurs at age thirteen for boys.

Calgary Urban Treaty Indian Alliance (CUTIA) An organization established in Calgary in 1973 to provide social services for Indigenous people in an urban setting. The organization was founded and run by Indigenous people and was funded by the Canadian government's Department of Indian Affairs. The Alliance supported the work of local social service agencies and was a model of autonomous program leadership by Indigenous people for their own communities, attracting the interest of Indigenous groups in other cities. In 1974, Indian Affairs withdrew funding, and members of the Alliance occupied Calgary's Indian Affairs office in protest. *See also* Department of Indian Affairs.

Catholic Mass The main religious service in the Roman Catholic Church, traditionally offered on Sundays, and for the dead or on special occasions.

Cold War The era of political hostility between the Soviet Union and the United States and their respective allies from the end of World War II until the fall of Eastern European Communist regimes in 1989. The Cold War era in America was characterized by a fear of Communist influences and the threat of imminent nuclear war. *See also* Communist.

Communist Based on the principles of communism, a political and economic theory advocating public ownership and shared control over a society's resources. Communism was rooted in the socialist writings of nineteenth-century philosopher and economist Karl Marx (1818–1883). In the twentieth century, several countries, including the Soviet Union, China, Korea and Vietnam, adopted totalitarian communist political structures that were characterized by oppression of opposition and state-control of property and resources. *See also* Cold War.

concentration camp A location in which people are held without recourse to rule of law, usually under difficult conditions. Under the Nazis, a large network of concentration camps was developed where prisoners — including Jews, Roma, homosexuals, political prisoners, prisoners of war, and others considered "undesirable" — were used as slave labour and provided with little food or other necessities, often resulting in death due to starvation, illness, exposure, beatings and execution. The camps were run by the SS, the elite police force of the Nazi regime that was responsible for security and for the enforcement of Nazi racial policies.

Conservative (Judaism) The religious practice of Jews that maintains elements of traditional Judaism while reinterpreting Jewish law to adapt to modern life. *See also* Orthodox; Reform.

death camps Killing centres established by the Nazis to murder designated groups of people on a highly organized, mass scale. *See also* Auschwitz; concentration camp; gas chamber.

Department of Indian Affairs A federal body established in 1755 in what is now Canada to manage the relationship between British colonials and Indigenous Peoples, their land and resources. In its early years, the department was responsible for negotiating treaties with Indigenous Peoples, making way for immigrants to settle the land. The department was renamed several times over the years, and in 2017 was replaced by two departments: Crown-Indigenous Relations and Northern Affairs, which oversees relationships between Indigenous Peoples and the government, including matters related to natural resources, self-governance and treaty rights; and Indigenous Services Canada, which oversees the services offered to Indigenous Peoples, such as water supplies and energy systems.

Frank, Anne (1929–1945) A German-Jewish teenager who spent twenty-five months in hiding with her family and four other people in Amsterdam during World War II, during which time she wrote a diary. Anne and her family were discovered and arrested on August 4, 1944, and were transported to Auschwitz-Birkenau. Anne died in Bergen-Belsen from typhus seven months later. Her diary has since been translated into more than seventy languages and was first published in English as *Anne Frank: The Diary of a Young Girl* (1952).

gas chamber A sealed room into which either carbon monoxide or Zyklon B, a poisonous gas, was emitted in order to kill people. The Nazis began experimenting with carbon monoxide gas in late 1939, using it to kill people with mental or physical disabilities. In mid-1941, they began using gas vans, sealed trucks that were filled with engine exhaust. Later that same year, the Nazis opened the first killing centre, Chelmno, in Poland, which used gas vans. Beginning in 1942, gas chambers were used at the killing centres of Belzec, Sobibor, Treblinka and Auschwitz. Smaller gas chambers were built at several concentration camps, including Stutthof, Mauthausen, Sachsenhausen and Ravensbrück. *See also* Auschwitz; death camps.

Gestapo (German; abbreviation of Geheime Staatspolizei, the Secret State Police) The Nazi regime's brutal political police that operated without legal constraints to deal with its perceived enemies. The Gestapo was formed in 1933 under Hermann Göring; it was taken over by Heinrich Himmler in 1934 and became a department within the SS in 1939. During the Holocaust, the Gestapo set up offices in Nazi-occupied countries and was responsible for rounding up Jews and sending them to concentration and death camps. They also arrested, tortured and deported those who resisted Nazi policies.

Hanukkah (also Chanukah; Hebrew; dedication) An eight-day festival of lights, usually celebrated in December, that commemorates the victory of the Jews against the Syrian-Greek empire in the second century BCE. The festival is celebrated with the lighting of an eight-branched candelabrum called a menorah, or chanukiah, in remembrance of the rededication of the Temple in Jerusalem and the miracle of one day's worth of oil burning for eight days of light.

Havdalah (Hebrew; separation) A Jewish ritual done at the end of the Sabbath and Jewish holidays, marking the separation between days of holiness and ordinary weekdays. During the Havdalah after the Sabbath, blessings are recited over a cup of wine, fragrant spices and a candle flame.

Heschel, Abraham Joshua (1907–1972) A leading American rabbi and theologian known for his presentation of a contemporary Jewish theology rooted in traditional Jewish thought. Heschel was born in Warsaw, Poland (then the Russian Empire), and received rabbinic ordination and a doctorate from the University of Berlin, where he taught until the Nazis deported him from Germany in 1938. From 1945 until his death, Heschel was a professor of Jewish ethics and mysticism at New York's Jewish Theological Seminary of America. He wrote several influential and widely read books on the philosophy of religion, spirituality, faith, prophecy and Jewish mysticism. Heschel believed that inner spiritual experience should be linked to social action and was active in the US civil rights movement in the 1960s.

Jewish Council (in German, Judenrat) A group of Jewish leaders appointed by the Nazis to administer the ghettos and carry out Nazi orders. The councils tried to provide social services to the Jewish population to alleviate the harsh conditions of the ghettos and maintain a sense of community. The councils were under Nazi control and faced difficult and complex moral decisions under brutal conditions — having to decide whether to cooperate with or resist Nazi demands, when refusal likely meant death — and they remain a contentious subject.

King, Jr., Martin Luther (1929–1968) American activist and Baptist minister who was a prominent leader in the movement to end racial segregation and discrimination in the United States in the 1950s and 1960s. His organization, Southern Christian Leadership Conference, promoted nonviolent resistance tactics, and King led or joined protest marches in support of equality and economic and civil rights, and in opposition to the Vietnam War. He wrote several books and numerous articles and was known for his eloquent and powerful speeches. King was awarded the Nobel Peace Prize in 1964 for his work in racial equality. He was assassinated in 1968.

Luther, Martin (1483–1546) German priest and theologian who led the Protestant Reformation. His antisemitic treatise *On the Jews and Their Lies* argued that Jews' property and writings should be destroyed, their synagogues burned, and that they should be persecuted, made to do hard labour and even murdered. Luther was successful in getting Jews expelled and prohibiting them from doing business in the Electorate of Saxony (now part of Germany and Poland).

Mechelen (also Malines) A city in Belgium where the Kazerne Dossin military base was located. It was used as a transit camp for Jews and Roma from 1942 to 1944. Over 25,000 Jews and several hundred Roma were deported from this site to Auschwitz-Birkenau and other camps.

Orthodox (Judaism) The religious practice of Jews for whom the observance of Judaism is rooted in the traditional rabbinical interpretations of the biblical commandments. Orthodox Jewish practice is characterized by strict observance of Jewish law and tradition, such as the prohibition to work on the Sabbath and certain dietary restrictions. *See also* Conservative; Reform.

Passover (in Hebrew, Pesach) An eight-day Jewish festival that takes place in the spring and commemorates the exodus of the Israelite slaves from Egypt. The festival begins with a lavish ritual meal called a seder, during which the story of the Exodus is told through the reading of a Jewish text called the Haggadah. During Passover, Jews refrain from eating any leavened foods. The name of the festival refers to God's "passing over" the houses of the Jews and sparing their lives during the last of the ten plagues, when the first-born sons of Egyptians were killed by God. *See also* seder.

Pentagon Papers (Officially "History of US Decision-Making in Vietnam, 1945–68") A top-secret government report commissioned by the US Secretary of Defense in 1967 to investigate the military and political involvement of the United States in the Vietnam War. The report was leaked to the press in 1971 by Daniel Ellsberg, one of its authors who opposed the Vietnam War and believed that the information should be available to the public. The published sections of the report revealed that the US government had misled the public about the United States' involvement and impact in the war.

Rabin, Yitzhak (1922–1995) Israeli soldier, ambassador and prime minister (1974–1977; 1992–1995). As prime minister, Rabin signed a peace treaty with Jordan and pursued political solutions to the ongoing conflict with the Palestinians, negotiating with the nationalist PLO (Palestine Liberation Organization) and signing several historic agreements with the Palestinian leadership. Rabin received the Nobel Peace Prize in 1994 and was assassinated at a peace rally in Tel Aviv by a Jewish extremist in 1995.

Reform (Judaism) (also known as Progressive Judaism, Liberal Judaism) A Jewish denomination that emerged in nineteenth-century Germany in response to Jewish emancipation and integration into secular culture. Reform Judaism focuses on adapting religious life to new social and political conditions, understanding Jewish law to be non-binding and emphasizing ethical and progressive elements of Jewish tradition and practice over ritual ones. *See also* Conservative; Orthodox.

Righteous Among the Nations A title given by Yad Vashem, the World Holocaust Remembrance Center in Jerusalem, to honour non-Jews who risked their lives to help save Jews during the Holocaust. A commission was established in 1963 to award the title. If a person fits certain criteria and the story is carefully checked, the honouree is awarded with a medal and certificate and is commemorated on the Wall of Honour at the Garden of the Righteous in Jerusalem.

Rosh Hashanah (Hebrew; New Year) The two-day autumn holiday that marks the beginning of the Jewish year and ushers in the High Holidays. It is celebrated with a prayer service and the blowing of the shofar (ram's horn), as well as festive meals that include symbolic foods such as an apple dipped in honey, which symbolizes the desire for a sweet new year.

seder (Hebrew; order) A ritual meal celebrated at the beginning of the festival of Passover. A traditional seder involves reading the Haggadah, which tells the story of the Israelite slaves' exodus from Egypt; drinking four cups of wine; eating matzah and other symbolic foods that are arranged on a special seder plate; partaking in a festive meal; and singing traditional songs. *See also* Passover.

Shabbat (Hebrew; Sabbath) The weekly day of rest beginning Friday at sunset and ending Saturday at nightfall, ushered in by the lighting of candles on Friday evening and the recitation of blessings over wine and challah (egg bread). A day of celebration as well as prayer, it is customary to eat three festive meals, attend synagogue services and refrain from doing any work or travelling.

Sudetenland The name used between 1919 and the end of World War II to refer to the region of Czechoslovakia that bordered on Germany and Austria and was inhabited primarily by ethnic Germans. The Sudetenland was annexed by Germany in October 1938 under the terms of the Munich Agreement.

ten Boom, Corrie (1892–1983) A member of the Dutch resistance who rescued Jews from the Nazis because of her religious belief in the equality of all people. She was imprisoned and held in a concentration camp for her rescue work and was recognized by Yad Vashem as Righteous Among the Nations in 1967. *See also* Righteous Among the Nations; Yad Vashem.

Torah (Hebrew; instruction) The first five books of the Hebrew Bible, also known as the Five Books of Moses or Chumash, the content of which is traditionally believed to have been revealed to Moses on Mount Sinai; or, the entire canon of the twenty-four books of the Hebrew Bible, referred to as the Old Testament in Christianity. Torah is also broadly used to refer to all the teachings that were given to the Jewish people through divine revelation or even through rabbinic writings (called the Oral Torah).

Vietnam War A war that was fought between the communist government of North Vietnam and its allies against a US-backed South Vietnam from 1954 to 1975. The war began after North Vietnam defeated the French colonial administration in Vietnam and tried to unify the country under a communist regime like that in the Soviet Union. The United States supported South Vietnam, with more that 500,000 US military personnel joining the fighting by 1969. The war resulted in a huge number of civilian and military casualties. North Vietnamese forces entered Saigon and North and South Vietnam were united to create the Socialist Republic of Vietnam in 1976. *See also* Cold War; Communist; Pentagon Papers.

Wiesel, Elie (1928–2016) A Romanian-born Jewish writer, professor and Holocaust survivor who was a human rights activist. Among numerous other prizes, Wiesel was awarded the Nobel Peace Prize in 1986. His most well-known book, *Night*, recounts his experience in Auschwitz and Buchenwald and is widely considered one of the most important works of Holocaust literature.

Yad Vashem Israel's official Holocaust memorial centre and the world's largest collection of information on the Holocaust, established in 1953. Yad Vashem, the World Holocaust Remembrance Center, is dedicated to commemoration, research, documentation and education about the Holocaust. The Yad Vashem complex in Jerusalem includes museums, sculptures, exhibitions, research centres and the Garden of the Righteous Among the Nations.

Photographs

1. Ben's maternal grandparents, Fanny and Julius Gerstl. Place and date unknown.
2. Ben's mother, Elsa. Place unknown, 1928.
3. Ben's father, Mathias. Place and date unknown.
4. Ben's parents, Mathias and Elsa, on their wedding day. Teplitz-Schönau (Teplice-Šanov), Czechoslovakia, 1930.

1 Ben's parents at an outing at the Elbe River. Czechoslovakia, 1934.
2 Ben with his mother. Teplitz-Schönau, Czechoslovakia, 1937.
3 Ben with his father and maternal grandfather. Teplitz-Schönau, 1938.
4 Ben with his mother. Brussels, Belgium, 1941.

Ben. Brussels, 1941.

1 Ben's rescuers, Minn Verschueren and Dr. Frantz Vandenheuvel, at their wedding. London, England, 1936.
2 Frantz wearing a Belgian army officer's uniform. Place and date unknown.
3 Minn's brother Albert, who provided Ben with false identity papers. The badge on his beret indicates that he was in the Free Belgian forces, the exiled Belgian army that fought the Nazis alongside the Allies. Date and place unknown.
4 Minn's parents, Monsieur et Madame Verschueren. Date and place unknown.

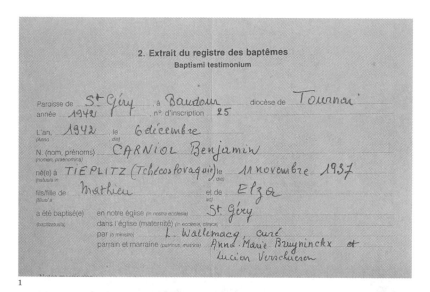

1 Ben's baptism card.
2 Ben with his rescuer, Aunt Minn. Baudour, Belgium, circa 1943.

1 Ben (right) playing soldiers with a friend. Baudour, circa 1943.
2 Ben posing with a Christmas tree, a Star of David ornament visible above him. Baudour, circa 1943.
3 Ben after the war. Baudour, June 1945.

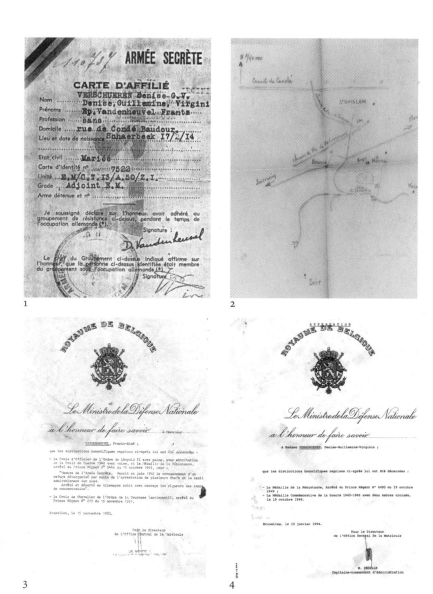

1 Document showing the affiliation of Frantz and Minn (Denise) in the Secret Army.
2 Map drawn by Frantz as part of a mission for the Secret Army.
3 & 4 Certificates from the Belgian government acknowledging Frantz and Minn for their work in the underground during World War II.

```
31.CARDOZO    ép. Gans          27 octobre 1900        ménagère
   Sophie                       Amsterdam
   C. VIII/99
32.CARELS     ep. Van Thijn     21 février 1889        ménagère
   Sophia                       Amsterdam
   C. VI/510  AB 1558
33.CARFUNKEL  ép. Honik         20 juin 1896           ménagère
   Beila                        Zolinika
   C. VIII/340  AB 4710
34.CARITON    ép. Torenhajm     27 juillet 1903        ménagère
   Lisa                         Odessa
   C. XI/1731
35.CARNI                        1888                   march.Ambul.
   Salomon Abraham              Vilhoma
   C. IX/448
36.CARNIOL                      1 février 1895         émpl.de bur.
   Mathias                      Berlad
   C. XVII/869
37.CARO       ép. Kerner        24 décembre 1912       ménagère
   Hélène                       Ritschenwalde
   C. II/918  AB 9647
38.CARO       ép. Ullmann       3 avril 1874           sans
   Bara                         Lobau
   C. XIV/131
```

1

GERSTL Epse. Echtg. : HIRSCHL	Berta	29.3.97	XXVI/110	31.7.44
GERSTL	Eduard	18.4.90	XXI/1147	31.7.43
GERSTL Epse. Echtg. : WELTSCH	Ella	27.12.93	XXVI/197	31.7.44
GERSTL Epse. Echtg. : CARNIOL	Else	3.11.01	XVI/154	31.10.42
GERSTL	Gisela	8.2.83	XXI/576	31.7.43
GERSTL	Hansi	2.1.13	XXII^A/592	20.9.43
GERSTL	Hilda-	voir zie : REICH Hilda		
GERSTL	Ilse	voir zie : URBACH Ilse		

2

1   Ben's father's name on a list of Jews sent by convoy to Auschwitz. He was prisoner 869 on transport XVII, sent from Mechelen on October 31, 1942. Courtesy of Arolsen Archives.

2   Ben's mother's name on a list of Jews sent by convoy to Auschwitz. She was prisoner 154 on transport XVI, sent from Mechelen on October 31, 1942. Courtesy of Arolsen Archives.

1

2

Ben at the Ottawa airport being greeted by his family. In back (left to right): Ben's grandfather Julius Gerstl; a teacher, Mrs. Fourny; Ben's cousin Ricky; the musician Eugene Kash, who accompanied Ben on the plane; and a stewardess, Madge Scogin. In front (left to right): Ben's grandmother Fanny Gerstl; Ben; Ben's aunt Greta; and his cousins Sid and Ed. August 26, 1947.

Ben with his Ottawa family and his rescuers. Left to right (front row, sitting): Minn; Ben's grandmother Fanny Gerstl; his grandfather Julius Gerstl; Frantz. Back row (left to right): Ben's cousin Ed; his aunt Greta; his cousin Sid; family friend Percival Price; Ben; and Ben's cousin Ricky. Ottawa, circa 1948.

1 Ben with his grandparents Fanny and Julius Gerstl. Ottawa, June 1949.
2 Minn and Frantz. Halifax, circa 1949.
3 Ben and Frantz. Ottawa, 1949.

Ben at his bar mitzvah. Ottawa, 1950.

1 Ben and Greta at the Expo 67 World Fair. Montreal 1967.
2 Ben with a group he volunteered with at the YMHA in Montreal. Circa 1970.

Ben and Rhona at their wedding. Montreal, 1971.

1 Ben and Rhona's wedding. Front (left to right): Greta, Frantz, Minn. Montreal, 1971.
2 Ben and his family at a dinner put on by the Jewish National Fund at which his adoptive mother, Greta Cohen, was honoured. In front (left to right): Ben's wife, Rhona; Ben; Ben's adoptive mother, Greta; Ben's adoptive brother Sid and his wife, Ruth. In back (left to right): Ben's adoptive brother Ed and his wife, Fern; and Ben's adoptive sister, Ricky, and her husband, Harry Cherney. Ottawa, 1971.

1 Ben and Rhona. Calgary, 1973.
2 Ben and his daughter Mira. Calgary, 1974.

1 Ben's daughter Mira with Minn and Frantz. Ottawa, circa 1976.
2 Ben's daughter Mira with Minn. Calgary, circa 1978.

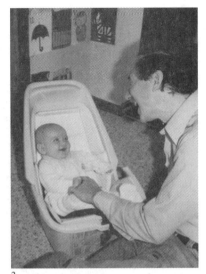

1 Ben with Mira. Calgary, circa 1978.
2 Ben with his daughter Naomi. Calgary, 1979.
3 Ben at a protest supporting social workers on strike. Oshawa, circa 1990.

Frantz and Minn. Ohain, Belgium, 1996.

1 Ben and Rhona whale watching in Quebec. Circa 1995.
2 Ben with his friend Elliot in Algonquin Park. Circa 2000.

1 Mira and Minn. Belgium, 1993.
2 Naomi (left) and Mira (right) with Minn. Belgium, circa 2000.

1 Ben with his family while visiting Florida. Left to right: Ben's adoptive brother Ed; Ed's wife, Fern; Ben's daughters, Naomi and Mira; Ben; Ben's adoptive brother Sid's son, Brian; Ben's wife, Rhona; Ben's adoptive brother Sid; Sid's wife, Barbara. Circa 2003.

2 Ben with Minn. Belgium, 2000.

1 Ben and Rhona with their daughter Naomi at her wedding. Toronto, 2012.
2 Ben's daughter Naomi with her husband, Brian, and children, Noah and Chloe. Toronto, 2019.
3 Ben's grandchildren Noah and Chloe. Toronto, 2022.

Ben. Toronto, 2023.

Index

abandonment, 65, 117–118, 141
Absolon, Kathy, 141
activism, Ben's: anti-Olympics organizing, 70–72; anti-poverty, 54, 67–74; Black voting rights, 54–58, 102, xxvii; and child survivors, Jewish, 102, xxvii–xxviii; decolonizing social work education, 113–119; Indigenous representation, 115–117; Indigenous rights, 85–88, 140; peace, 61–64, 136, 137–138; as resistance to suffering, 91; support of protests for Missing and Murdered Indigenous Women and Girls, 125–126
Albert, Jim (Elder), 121
Alissi, Al, 49–50, 65
Allied forces: American soldiers, Ben's memories of, 61, 63; bombing Baudour, 9–10, 13–14; celebrating liberation (Baudour), 17; flying over Baudour, 105–106; in war movie, 14
Alta House (Cleveland), 49–51, 61, 65–66
Anishinaabe water ceremony, 124–125
antisemitism, 35–37, 41, 45–47, 91
Antone, Bob (Robert), 123
Assembly of First Nations, 131
Auschwitz, 102–103, 110–111
Awnjibinayseekwe (Banakonda), 121–126, 133
Baldwin, James, 54
Banakonda Kennedy-Kish (Bell), 121–126, 133, 141
bar mitzvah, 28–29
Bastien, Helen (welfare advocate), 67
Baudour, Belgium: American soldiers in, 61, 63; Belgian resistance in, 8; Ben living as Catholic, xx; bombing of, 9–10, 13–14; Catholic church, 7–8; Catholic school, 7; celebrating liberation, 17–18; foreign forces in, 10, 13; home in, 6; stream in, 15–16; train ride to, 6
Belgium, 5–6, 8, xix, xx. *see also*

Baudour, Belgium; Brussels, Belgium
Berman, Paul, xxviii
Black Lives Matter, 91
Black militants, 57
Black voter registration, US, 54–56, 57–58, 102, xxvii
blame machines, 130–131, 135, 142
British Mandate Palestine. *see* Israel
Brussels, Belgium, 3, 11, 97, 101, 105–107
Buddhists, persecution of, 62
Calgary, Alberta, 79, 81–85, 89, 95–97, xxv
Calgary Urban Treaty Indian Alliance, 85–86
Calls to Action, TRC, 131
Canadian Association of Schools of Social Work (CASSW), 113, 116–118
Canadian government, systems of, 18, 67, 131, xxii
cantors, 26–27, 40
capitalism, 133
Carleton University, School of Social Work, 121
Carmichael, Stokely, 54
Carniol, Ben. *see also* activism, Ben's
—early life, Belgium: adopting Catholicism, 7–8; airplane explosion, 11; American soldiers in Baudour, 61, 63; bombings in Baudour, 9–10, 13–14; under care of Minn and Frantz, 5, xx; Catholic school, 7; celebrating liberation, 17–18; confession of Jewish identity, 8; flight to Belgium, xix; hiding Jewish identity, 6–7; parents leave on "vacation," 3, xx; sadness about parents, 15–16; streetcar checkpoint (German), 12; war movie in school, 14–15
—early life, Ottawa: adoption, 24; antisemitic doctor, 36–37; antisemitic neighbour, fight with, 35–36; arrival, 19–20; bar mitzvah, 28–29; cross over bed, 20–21, xxii–xxiii; gendered labour in household, 76–77; and grandfather's grief, supporting, 31–33; and grief, processing, xxiv; home in Ottawa, 20; and hope of parents' return, 24; keeping surname, 24; Minn's visit and Catholicism, 27–28; reclaiming Judaism, 25–29, 140; and shul with grandparents, 26–27; synagogue, first experience of, 25–26
—adult life, Calgary: birth of daughter, Naomi Tamara, 83–84; birth of daughter Mira Elsa, 81–82; Mira Elsa at emergency, 82–83; tense visit with Frantz and Minn, 95–97; traumatic memory, 84, xxv
—adult life, Cleveland: Alta House, job at, 49–51; Black American experience, education in, 53–54; Black voter registration, 54–56;

Martin Luther King, Jr., 57–58; questioning assumptions about US, 65
—adult life, Montreal: anti-Olympics organizing, 69–72; Rhona, dating and engagement, 74–77; Rhona, marriage to, 77–79; social work school, McGill, 44, 74; welfare advocacy, 67–69
—adult life, Toronto: Jewish persecution, learning histories of, 45–47; law school, University of Toronto, 39, 43–44; mourning adoptive mother, 99–100; questioning life path, 42–43; return to, 99; shaking episode, 41–42; visiting different synagogues, 40–41
—inner life: abandonment, childhood, 117–118; affected by Cleveland, 66; capitalism, questioning, 133; and decolonizing social work education, 116; God's presence, 81–83, 100–101, 104, 118; grieving and communing with birth parents, 100–104, xxvi; Indigenous teachings and pathways to the sacred, 127; on miracles, 139–142; parents at Auschwitz, learning of, 109–111; peace institutions, Israel-Palestine conflict, 136–138; and Rabbi Heschel's teachings, 81, 92–93; repressed emotions of Holocaust, 84; settler identity, 128; spirituality and progressive politics, 94; suffering, Jewish teachings on, 90–91; and Vietnam War, 65; and welfare advocacy as meaningful, 67
—social justice: to amplify parents' resistance, 102; anti-Olympics organizing, 70–72; anti-racism as empowerment, 66; anti-war protests, 62–64; call to seek, 142; as central to Jewish faith, 93; and civil rights movement, 53–59; decolonizing social work education, 113–119; drive to widen strategy of, 91; emergent interest in, 39–40, 43, 47; failure, sense of, 72; Indigenous rights activism, 85–88, 140; motivations to, 1–2; overview, xxvii–xxviii; welfare advocacy, 67–69
Carniol, Elsa (birth mother): Ben mourning and communing with, 100–102; in Ben's bar mitzvah speech, 29; daughter named after, 81; departure from Ben, 4–6; grandfather grieving, 31; leaving on "vacation," xx; sent to Auschwitz, 110
Carniol, Joseph (uncle), 104
Carniol, Malvine (aunt Molly), 104
Carniol, Mathias (birth father): Ben mourning and communing with, 100–102; in Ben's bar mitzvah speech, 29; daughter named after, 83; departure from Ben, 4–6; in historical record, 109–110; leaving on "vacation,"

xx; sent to Auschwitz, 110
Carniol, Mira Elsa (daughter), 81–82, 96, 105, 138
Carniol, Naomi Tamara (daughter), 83–84, 96, 138, xxv
Case Critical: Social Services and Social Justice in Canada (Kennedy-Kish et al.), 133
Catholicism, 6–7, 21, 26–28, 42, 46, 50, 132, xx–xxiii
Chang, Jim, 66, 73–74, 78
cheder (Hebrew classes), 27, 41
child survivors, Jewish. *see also* genocide; trauma: and activism, adult, xxvii–xxviii; as parents, xxv–xxvi; in care of near-strangers, 5, xx; emotional conflicts of re-Judaicization, xxiii; grief as adults, 41–42, xxvi; hiding as Christians, 6–7, xx–xxi; parents returning, hope of, 24, xxiv–xxv; as postwar global diaspora, xxii; reclaiming of, postwar, 19–20, xxi–xxiii; unaware of danger, xix–xx
civil rights movement, 51, 54, 57–58, 73
Cleveland, Ohio: anti-Black police chief fired, 63; anti-Black racism, reactions to, 53; Ben's Alta House job, 49; Black voter registration, 54–56; Carl Stokes elected mayor, 58, 73; Martin Luther King, Jr. in, 57–58; neighbourhood council, 50–51; newspaper coverage of anti-war protests, 64
Cohen, Ed (cousin, adoptive brother), 20, 25–26
Cohen, Greta (mother's sister, adoptive mother): as Aunt Greta, 23; Ben's bar mitzvah speech, 29; death and mourning of, 99–100; letter from Minn's father, 18–19; as Mum, 24; on pathways to understanding God, 127; at synagogue, 26. *see also* Correspondence section, 143–173
Cohen, Ricky (cousin, adoptive sister): Ben as natural speaker, 29; as Ben's translator, 20, 23; at grandfather's grief episode, 32–33; pride in Ben's Judaism, 28; reaction to Ben's fight with neighbour, 35–36; at synagogue, 26
Cohen, Sid (cousin, adoptive brother), 21, 96, 105
Cohen, Yisrael Elliot, 109
Cold War, 62, xxvii
colonialism, violence of, 127, 129, 140
compassion, 47, 92. *see also* empathy; suffering
concentration camps, 46–47, 101, 102–103
Conservative (Judaism), 40
convents, Catholic, xxi
creation stories, 127
crosses, Catholic, 20–21, 27, xxii–xxiii

Czechoslovakia (Sudetenland), 5–6, xix
death camps. *see* concentration camps
dehumanization, 45, 93, 131–132
democracy, 61–62, 136, 138, 140
demonstrations, 62–64, 69, 72 86–88, 125–126, 132, 136. *see also* activism, Ben's
denominations, Jewish, 40–41. *see also* Conservative; Orthodox; Reform
Department of Indian Affairs, 85–88
Doctrine of Discovery, 131–132
Drapeau, Jean (Montreal mayor), 70–71
Dumont, Jim (Elder), 122, 123, 127
Ed. *see* Cohen, Ed (cousin, adoptive brother)
Elders, Indigenous, 113–115, 121–123, 127, 140
Elsa (birth mother). *see* Carniol, Elsa (birth mother)
empathy, 129–130, 132, 135, 140, 142. *see also* compassion; suffering
English, Ben learning, 23
factories of murder, 46–47, 101. *see also* concentration camps
father, birth. *see* Carniol, Mathias (birth father)
fear, Ben's: of cantor, 26; of communism, 65; and Frantz's arrest, 9; and German soldiers, 11–12; of mourning parents, 103–104; moving beyond, 139–140; of police violence, 86–87; and postwar trauma, 1, 100, 103–104, xxvi
Fekete, Ida (mother's sister), 18. *see also* Correspondence section, 143–173
First Lady Nation: Stories by Aboriginal Women (Eastman), 130
First Nations Technical Institute (FNTI), 121, 122
Frank, Anne, 45
Frantz. *see* Vandenheuvel, Frantz
Freedom Summer (1964), xxvii
French, Ben learning, 3
Friedman, Paul, xxiii
future, building better, 58, 63, 107, 138, 142
gas chamber. *see* concentration camps
gender equality, 76–77, 84, 93
genocide. *see also* child survivors, Jewish: and dehumanization, 45, 47, 93; of Indigenous Peoples, 122, 126, 127–129, 132; of Jews, xxiv, xxvii, 1, 54, 92, 132, 140, 141
German, Ben learning, 27
German soldiers (Brussels), 11–12. *see also* soldiers
Gerstl, Fanny (maternal grandmother), 19, 23, 26–27, 31–32, 140. *see also* Correspondence section, 143–173
Gerstl, Julius (maternal grandfather), 19, 20–21, 23, 26–27, 29, 31–33. *see also* Correspondence

section, 143–173
Gestapo, 9–10, 97
God, presence of. *see also* love: and accusations at CASSW, 118; and birth of daughter, Mira Elsa, 81–82; and birth of daughter, Naomi Tamara, 83; and miracles of healing, 141; in mourning birth parents, 100–101, 104
Greater Montreal Anti-Poverty Coordinating Committee, 67–74
greed, 90–91, 94, 139
Greta. *see* Cohen, Greta (mother's sister, adoptive mother)
grief: and Carniol family, 31, 42, xxiv; of grandfather (maternal), 31–33; processing, 24, 41–42, 103–104, xxiv. *see also* Correspondence section, 143–173
Grossmama. *see* grandmother (maternal)
Grosspapa. *see* grandfather (maternal)
guest–host relationship, 128, 140
Gutnick, Nelson, 85–87
Haggadah, 25, 77–78, 79
Hannukah, 25
Havdalah, 89
Hebrew classes (cheder), 27, 41
Hebrew University, 109
Heschel, Abraham Joshua (Rabbi), 81, 92–93
Hill, Gus, 141
Hill, Lori, 141
Hillel (Jewish student organization), 61
Holy Blossom Temple, Toronto, 138
hope, 56, 88, 101–102, 116, 125, 136–137, 139
host families, wartime, xxi
Hough, Cleveland, 53
household labour, division of, 76–77, 84
housing justice, 50–51, 66
human nature as excuse, 1, 53–54, 65, 66, 89, 94, 139–140
humour, 33, 74, 88, 123. *see also* joy; laughter
identification papers, 6, 12
indemnification program (West German), xxiv
Indian Affairs Office, Calgary, 85
Indian Residential School System, 114, 130. *see also* genocide; trauma
Indigenous ceremony, 113, 115, 124–125
Indigenous Elders, 113–115, 121–123, 127, 140
Indigenous faculty, 115–116
Indigenous knowledge and practice, 113, 114–115, 122
Indigenous rights, 85–87, 91, 127–128, 132, xxvii
Indigenous song, 124, 126
Indigenous thriving, 130
injustice. *see also* activism; Carniol, Ben; justice; social work: Heschel on, 92; and Indigenous Peoples in Canada, 85–87, 131–132; and racism, 45, 66;

resisting, 1, 107
Israel, xxii
Israeli government, 136–137
Israel-Palestine conflict, 135–136
Jeremiah (Jewish prophet), 93
Jewish prophets, ancient, 92–93
Jewish Reform movement, Calgary, 89
Johnson, Lyndon B. administration, 61, 66
joy, 17, 77, 84, 124, xxi
Judaism: Ben's return to, 25–26, 47, 140; and connection to community, 74; and grieving loss, 104; history of persecution, 45–46; inclusive forms of, 93; living in Cohen family, 25; right-wing, 135–136; teachings, 135; and teaching conversion course, 89–90; various denominations, 40–41
justice, 1–2, 40–43, 66, 91, 139–142. *see also* activism; Carniol, Ben; injustice; social work
Kaddish prayer, 99–100, 104
Kainai (Blood) Chiefs, 86
Kash, Eugene (plane passenger), 19–20
Katadotis, Peter, 68
Kathy (Jim Chang's partner), 74, 78
Kennedy-Kish, Banakonda (Bell), 121–126, 133, 141
Kerner Commission report (on racism), 66
Kiikeewanniikaan (Indigenous healing lodge), 123

King, Jr., Martin Luther, 54, 56–57, 63, 92
Koleszar-Green, Ruth, 128
Kristallnacht, 5
Ku Klux Klan, 53
land-based education, 122–126
landlords, unjust, 50–51, 72–73
laughter, 5, 29, 69, 79, 84, 123, xxv. *see also* humour; joy
Laurentian University, social work, 114
law, biases of, 43
Lazarovitch, Rosa (paternal great-grandmother), 104
Leduc, Timothy, 141
Liebman, Marcel, 109–110
Lingfield, England (orphanage), xxiv
Little Italy, Cleveland, 49–51, 66
Longboat, Dan, 123
love: family, 23, 27–28, 32–33, 83, 99–104, 140–141; power of, 139; religious, 81, 83, 91, 135; romantic, 74, 77, 110
Luther, Martin (Protestant), 46
Maritime School of Social Work, 114
Mathias (birth father). *see* Carniol, Mathias (birth father)
McGill University, social work, 44, 66, 74
McKay, Monica, 116
Mechelen (Malines) transit camp, 110
media representations: of anti-war protests, 64; of Calgary Indian

Affairs office occupation, 86, 87; of Calgary police chief, 87; of Missing and Murdered Indigenous Women and Girls protest, 126; of Olympics in Montreal (1976), 70, 71–72; of Vietnam War, 61, 65; of youth centres (Montreal), 72
memory: of birth parents, 100–102; flashback to wartime Baudour, 105–106; lapses, 1; of Martin Luther King, Jr., 56; traumatic, 1, xxv
#MeToo movement, 91
military violence, 61–63, 72, 102, 107, 136–137. *see also* soldiers
Minn. *see* Vandenheuvel, Minn
Mons, Belgium, 10
Montreal, Quebec, 36, 44, 67–74, 75
Montreal Council of Social Agencies, 66–67
Moore, Dorothy, 114, 118
Moses, 90
mother, adoptive. *see* Cohen, Greta (mother's sister, adoptive mother)
mother, birth. *see* Carniol, Elsa (birth mother)
music: Black musicians, 54; Indigenous song, 124, 126; in Jewish worship, 25–27, 40, 78–79, 82; Mathias Carniol chanting, 110; orchestra musician, 20; and voter registration truck, 56–57
National Film Board, 68

nature, beauty of, 77, 106, 139
Nazi collaborators, 18
Nelson Small Legs, Jr., 85, 88, 89, 91
neo-Nazis, 64
New York City, 63–64
Night of Broken Glass, 5
nonviolent protest, 57, 63–65, 126, 136
nuclear weapons, 137
Œuvre de secours aux enfants (OSE), xxi
Ohio House of Representatives, 54
oil and gas industries, 128, 132–133, 140
Olympics, Summer 1976 (Montreal), 70–72
orphanages (Jewish child survivors), xxv
Orthodox (Judaism), 40, 76, 81, 136
Ottawa, Ontario, 19–36, xxii
Parallel Institute, 68
parents, imagining experiences of, 103, 111
Passover, 25, 77–79
peace, institutions of, 136–138
Pentagon Papers, 62
Phillips, Aida (Ben's mother-in-law), 76, 79
Phillips, Jimmy (Ben's brother-in-law), 78
Phillips, Rhona (life partner): Ben's blind date with, 74; Ben's continued care for, 142; Ben's engagement to, 75; birth of daughter, Mira Elsa, 81–82; birth of daughter, Naomi Tamara, 83–84;

family of, 76–79, 82; at Frantz
and Minn's, Ottawa, 95–97; in
peace movements, 137; teaching
conversion course, 89–90
Phillips, Sydney (Ben's father-in-
law), 76, 77–78, 79
Piikani (Peigan) Chiefs, 86
police: in council chamber,
Montreal municipality, 72; and
Indian Affairs office occupation,
87; at Missing and Murdered
Indigenous Women and Girls
protest, 126; and murders of
Nazi collaborators, 18; at New
York anti-war protests, 64; and
reports of threats to Martin
Luther King, Jr., 63; and War
Measures Act (Montreal), 72; at
welfare offices, 68–69; youth in
conflict with (Cleveland), 49
poverty. *see also* activism: Ben's
assumptions about, 68; Ben's
awareness of, growing, 39–40,
43; and Ben's welfare advocacy,
67–69; as pervasive in US, 65;
Rabbi Heschel on, 92–93
Putin, Vladimir, 138
Quebec Ministry of Health and
Social Services, 72
Rabin, Yitzhak, 136
racism: anti-Black, Canada, 73;
anti-Black, Cleveland, 53–54, 63,
129; anti-Indigenous, Canada,
127–128, 129; anti-Indigenous
mayor, Calgary, 86–87; Black
militant defiance of, 57; and

Doctrine of Discovery, 132;
Heschel's response to, 92; and
the Holocaust, 45, 54; and housing, 72–73; Kerner Commission
report, 66; neo-Nazis, 64; as
pervasive in US, 65; systemic
racism, 53, 66; and White allies,
58
Rappaport, Morton, 110
reclaiming Jewish children, xxi–xxii
Reform (Judaism), 40, 89
re-Judaicization, xxi, xxiii
religions, respect for all, 127, 142
religious extremism, 135–136
repression, emotional, 41–42,
103–104, 117. *see also* trauma
resistance, 1, 101, 107, xxvi. *see also*
activism; injustice
Rhona. *see* Phillips, Rhona (life
partner)
Ricky. *see* Cohen, Ricky (cousin,
adoptive sister)
Righteous Among the Nations, 107
Riley, Barbara (Elder, Waubauno
Kwe), 113–115
Romania, 104
Rosh Hashanah, 26
Roy Little Chief, 85, 87
Ryan, Joan, 86
Ryerson University. *see* Indian
Residential School System;
Toronto Metropolitan
University
Sainte-Agathe, Quebec, 76
seders, 25, 77–78. *see also* Passover
self-sacrifice, 88–89, 109–110

settler occupation, 127–128, 140
Shabbat, 25, 27, 89, 109–110
Shalom Disarmament, 138
shul and synagogue, 25–29, 40–41, 99–104
Sid. *see* Cohen, Sid (cousin, adoptive brother)
Siksik (Blackfoot) Chiefs, 86
Silver, Susan, 121
slavery, 54, 90, 131
smudge ceremonies, 113, 115
snuff box, 27
social justice. *see* activism; Carniol, Ben
social work, Ben's work in. *see also* poverty: anti-racist, 114; and community development, Cleveland, 49–51; education in, 74, xxvii; and learning from Black social workers, 53; and Martin Luther King, Jr., 57; at Montreal Council of Social Agencies, 66, 74; motivations to pursue, 44, 102
social work education, Ben's work in: Aboriginal Advisory Council, 116; hope of teaching, 74; Indigenous content, greater, 115–116; Indigenous educator caucus, CASSW, 116, 118; land-based education, 121–126; spirit as first, 123–124; teaching, University of Calgary, 79, 113
soldiers, 6, 10–14, 17, 61–62, 72, 110. *see also* military violence
Southern Christian Leadership Conference, 54
Spirit, 123–124, 127, 140, 141
spirituality, 93–94, 123–124, 126–127
Standing Rock land defenders, 91
State of Israel, Declaration of Independence, 137
Stokes, Carl, 54–55, 58, 63, 73
Stoney-Nakoda Chiefs, 86
student movement (1968), xxvii–xxviii
Sudetenland, 5, xix
suffering: and blame machines, 135; and empathy, 1, 47, 129–130, 132; Heschel's teachings on, 92–93; human responsibility to stop, 93; Jewish teachings on, 89–91
sukkah, 89
Summer Olympics (1976, Montreal), 70–72
systemic racism, 53, 66. *see also* racism
tallis (prayer shawl), 25–26, 101, 103
teachings, Indigenous, 114–115, 124–125
ten Boom, Corrie, 45
Teplitz-Schönau (Teplice-Šanov), Czechoslovakia, 5–6, xix
terra nullius, 131
Three Fires Midewiwin Lodge, 122
Timmins, Vivian, 130
Torah, 28–29, 82, 135–136
Toronto, Ontario, 39–44, 95, 99, 103, 114–118, 132, 138–139
Toronto Metropolitan University, social work, 114–118, 121
trauma: intergenerational

Indigenous, 122, 129–130, 141; postwar Jewish, 47, 97, 132, 140, xxv
Treaty 7, Indigenous Chiefs of, 86–87
Trent University, Indigenous Environmental Studies and Sciences, 123
Trudeau, Justin, 132
Truth and Reconciliation Commission (TRC), 131
Tsuut'ina (Sarcee) Chiefs, 86
Tyendinaga Mohawk Territory, 122–123, 125
Ukraine, invasion of, 138
United Nations Relief and Rehabilitation Administration (UNRRA), xxi
United Nations Security Council, 138
University of Calgary, 79, 85–86, 113
University of Connecticut, School of Social Work, 65
University of Toronto, law school, 39
Urban Calling Last, 85
Vandenheuvel, Albert, 4, 5
Vandenheuvel, Frantz: arrest and condemnation by Gestapo, 9–10; Ben left in care of, 5, 140, xx; Ben's first impression of, 4; death of, 105; liberation and celebration of, 17–18; move to Halifax, 24; recognized as Righteous Among the Nations, 107; relocation to Canada, 19, xxii; residing in Ottawa, 79; return to Belgium, 97; saving Nazi collaborator, 18; tense visit with in Ottawa, 95–97; underground resistance, Belgian, 5, 96–97; visiting Ben in Ottawa, 27
Vandenheuvel, Minn: and Ben in bomb shelter, 13–14; Ben left in care of, 5, 140, xx; and Ben's Catholicism (Ottawa), 27–28; Ben's first impression of, 4; Ben's gratitude expressed to, 106–107; celebrating liberation, 17; cross for Ben, 21; crying with Ben over parents, 15; death of, 107; as devout Catholic, 7, 28; and Frantz's arrest, 9–10; move to Halifax, 24; recognized as Righteous Among the Nations, 107; relocation to Canada, 19, xxii; residing in Ottawa, 79; return to Belgium, 97; tense visit with in Ottawa, 95–97; underground resistance, Belgian, 5
Vatican and Doctrine of Discovery, 132
Verschuerens (neighbours, parents of Minn), 3–5
victim blaming, 47
Vietnam War, 61–63, 65, 102, 137, xxvii
violence, military, 61–63, 72, 102, 107, 136–137
voting registration, Black (US), 54–56, 57–58, 102, xxvii
Walpole Island, Ontario, 113

War Measures Act, 72
wartime host families, xxi
water ceremony, Anishinaabe, 124–125
water protectors, women as, 124
Waubauno Kwe (Riley, Barbara), 113–115
welfare advocacy (Montreal), 67–69
Wet'suwet'en Hereditary Chiefs, 132
White allies (anti-racist), 58
Wiesel, Elie, 45
Wilfred Laurier University, Faculty of Social Work, 140
Yad Vashem, World Holocaust Remembrance Center, 107
YMCA/YMHA, Montreal, 74
youth centres, conditions of (Montreal), 72

The Azrieli Foundation was established in 1989 to realize and extend the philanthropic vision of David J. Azrieli, C.M., C.Q., M.Arch. The Foundation's mission is to support a wide spectrum of initiatives in education and research. The Azrieli Foundation is an active supporter of programs in the fields of education, the education of architects, scientific and medical research, and the arts. The Azrieli Foundation's many initiatives include: the Holocaust Survivor Memoirs Program, which collects, preserves, publishes and distributes the written memoirs of survivors in Canada; the Azrieli Institute for Educational Empowerment, an innovative program successfully working to keep at-risk youth in school; the Azrieli Fellows Program, which promotes academic excellence and leadership on the graduate level at Israeli universities; the Azrieli Music Project, which celebrates and fosters the creation of high-quality new Jewish orchestral music; and the Azrieli Neurodevelopmental Research Program, which supports advanced research on neurodevelopmental disorders, particularly Fragile X and Autism Spectrum Disorders.